America's Founding Fathers

JOHN ADAMS

Creating a Nation

Zachary Kent

Enslow Publishers, Inc.
40 Industrial Road   PO Box 38
Box 398   Aldershot
Berkeley Heights, NJ 07922   Hants GU12 6BP
USA   UK
http://www.enslow.com

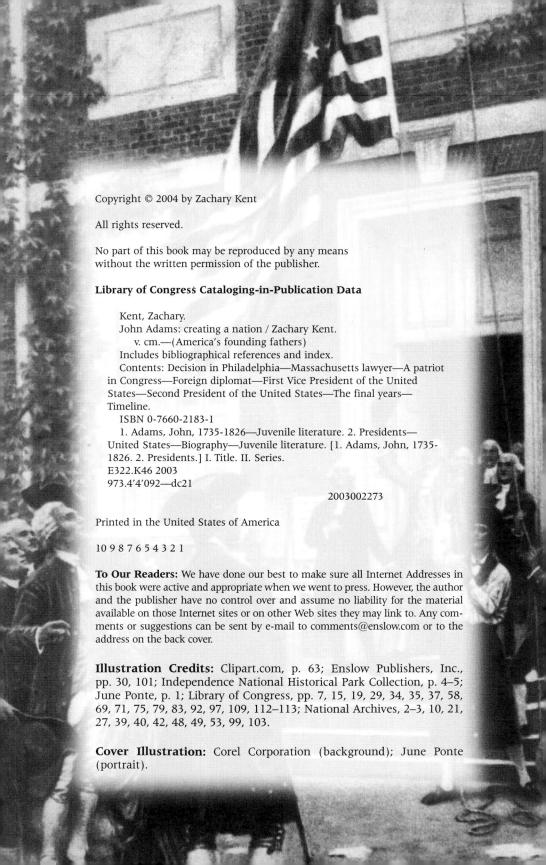

Library of Congress Cataloging-in-Publication Data

Kent, Zachary.
John Adams: creating a nation / Zachary Kent.
    v. cm.—(America's founding fathers)
Includes bibliographical references and index.
    Contents: Decision in Philadelphia—Massachusetts lawyer—A patriot
in Congress—Foreign diplomat—First Vice President of the United
States—Second President of the United States—The final years—
Timeline.
    ISBN 0-7660-2183-1
    1. Adams, John, 1735-1826—Juvenile literature. 2. Presidents—
United States—Biography—Juvenile literature. [1. Adams, John, 1735-
1826. 2. Presidents.] I. Title. II. Series.
E322.K46 2003
973.4′4′092—dc21

                                        2003002273

Printed in the United States of America

10 9 8 7 6 5 4 3 2 1

To Our Readers: We have done our best to make sure all Internet Addresses in
this book were active and appropriate when we went to press. However, the author
and the publisher have no control over and assume no liability for the material
available on those Internet sites or on other Web sites they may link to. Any com-
ments or suggestions can be sent by e-mail to comments@enslow.com or to the
address on the back cover.

Illustration Credits: Clipart.com, p. 63; Enslow Publishers, Inc.,
pp. 30, 101; Independence National Historical Park Collection, p. 4–5;
June Ponte, p. 1; Library of Congress, pp. 7, 15, 19, 29, 34, 35, 37, 58,
69, 71, 75, 79, 83, 92, 97, 109, 112–113; National Archives, 2–3, 10, 21,
27, 39, 40, 42, 48, 49, 53, 99, 103.

Cover Illustration: Corel Corporation (background); June Ponte
(portrait).

Contents

Colonial Philadelphia, Pennsylvania

Decision in Philadelphia

RAINCLOUDS DARKENED the sky over Philadelphia, Pennsylvania, on the hot summer day of July 1, 1776. Delegates to the Second Continental Congress excitedly gathered at the Pennsylvania State House. They mopped their faces with handkerchiefs and anxiously whispered back and forth. For a year, American revolutionaries had been at war with Great Britain. Just three weeks earlier, Virginia delegate Richard Henry Lee had made a formal suggestion. He had asked that the thirteen American colonies declare their independence from Great Britain. On this day, Lee's motion for independence would finally be debated.

Dickinson and Adams

At ten o'clock in the morning, John Hancock, president of the Congress, knocked a gavel on his desk. The room fell quiet as delegate John Dickinson of Pennsylvania stood beside Hancock's chair. Dickinson represented the members of Congress who were against declaring independence. Addressing his fellow delegates, Dickinson insisted that the colonies were too weak to declare independence from Great Britain. Such a declaration, Dickinson warned, would be "to brave the storm in a skiff [boat] made of paper."[1]

Dickinson finished his speech and sat down. His listeners remained silent. Perhaps they heard the sound of rain as it began to fall outside. It seemed no one in the hall was willing to answer Dickinson, until finally John Adams rose to his feet. The balding forty-year-old Massachusetts delegate stood five feet seven inches tall and had a round-shaped body. He looked around the room with his sharp blue eyes and prepared to make what may be considered the most important speech of his life.

When he began at last, Adams talked with steadiness and complete knowledge, making the argument for independence. Virginia delegate Thomas Jefferson later recalled that Adams's speech was "not graceful nor elegant, nor remarkably fluent [smooth]," but that he spoke "with a power of thought and expression that moved us from our seats."[2] New Jersey delegate Richard Stockton later exclaimed that Adams was the hero of the day, "the man to whom the country is most indebted for the great measure of independency."[3] For two hours without pausing, Adams spoke his heart and mind. No one took notes during the speech. It is unknown exactly what Adams said. But his words surely had an impact. When he took his seat at last, it was decided that the final vote for independence would be made the next day.

Pennsylvania delegate John Dickinson spoke at the Second Continental Congress for the delegates against independence from Great Britain.

The Historic Vote

The rain continued on July 2, 1776, the day of the independence vote. Adams and the other delegates soon sensed how the vote would go. At the last minute, Delaware delegate Caesar Rodney arrived, his riding boots and spurs streaked with mud. Rodney carried instructions from Delaware that its delegates should vote for independence. The South Carolina delegates also announced a shift for independence.

Even more important, Adams noticed, was the fact that Pennsylvania delegates John Dickinson and Robert Morris chose to be absent that day. Adams knew Pennsylvania's remaining delegates were sure to vote for independence, too. In the end, twelve colonies chose independence. Only New York's delegates abstained from voting. They did not vote either yes or no, but at a later date would decide yes. The great decision was made. On July 2, 1776, the American colonies declared their independence from Great Britain.

A Mistaken Prediction

On July 3, 1776, John Adams wrote a letter to his wife, Abigail, describing the thrilling vote for independence. "The second day of July 1776," he predicted, "will be the most memorable epocha [date] in the history of America. I . . . believe that it will be celebrated by succeeding generations as the great anniversary festival."[4] But Adams got the date wrong. July 4, the day Congress officially adopted the Declaration of Independence, is the day Americans celebrate as Independence Day.

Public Celebrations

Acceptance of the Declaration of Independence on July 4, 1776, marked the birth of a new nation, the United States of America. On July 8, a large crowd gathered in the yard of the Pennsylvania State House (called Independence Hall today). They listened as the declaration was read in public for the first time. When they learned the news, the crowd broke into wild cheering. Soon bonfires blazed at street corners in celebration. Some people excitedly climbed into church towers to ring the bells. "The Bells rung all Day, and almost all Night," Adams wrote. "Even the chimes chimed away!"[5]

Adams could be proud of the part he had played in winning the independence vote. He worked hard to persuade his fellow delegates to join him in the struggle for independence. Adams showed a great knowledge of history and governments in making his arguments. The Massachusetts lawyer had served the public and the nation all of his life. "I have a Zeal in my Heart, for my Country and her Friends, which I cannot smother or conceal," he once exclaimed.[6]

John Adams belongs to a special group of Americans. They have come to be known as the founding fathers. During the 1770s and 1780s, the founding fathers created a new and independent nation—the United States of America.

John Adams (pictured) was thrilled when the United States declared its independence in July 1776.

The creation of the United States was truly remarkable. It was a revolution, in fact. It seemed to turn the entire world upside down. Such a swift, complete, and surprisingly successful change in government had never occurred before in all of history.

The founding fathers were average people: lawyers, farmers, doctors, and merchants. They made great personal sacrifices to establish their dream of America. They defied Great Britain's King George III and risked their lives by signing the Declaration of Independence. After that, England regarded them as rebels and traitors. The founding fathers remained true to their revolutionary cause through eight hard years of war. And when the fighting ended, they boldly designed the Constitution. That set of laws remains the foundation of our national government. It is a democratic government, in which the people—not kings, dictators, or tyrants—make the laws.

With the passage of time, the founding fathers have become legendary American heroes. Taken together, they are a symbol of the greatness, wisdom, and the courage it took to form the United States. John Adams said the founding fathers were "present at the creation."[7]

John Adams was a signer of the Declaration of Independence. He was one of the nation's first diplomats in Europe, then the first vice president of the United States. He later became the second president of the United States. These many services easily earn Adams his place among America's founding fathers. Yet he remained critical of himself all of his life. "I am but an ordinary man," he insisted, "The times alone have [chosen me for] fame. . . ."[8]

Massachusetts Lawyer

THE FIVE-ROOM HOUSE of John Adams, Sr.,
and Susanna Boylston Adams stood beside the
Plymouth highway in Braintree, Massachusetts.
The town of Braintree was located about eight
miles south of Boston near the shore of
Massachusetts Bay. It was there that their first
child, John, was born on October 30, 1735. In the
years that followed, two other sons joined the
growing family, Peter in 1738 and Elihu in 1741.

John Adams, Sr., was a farmer, a deacon in
the local church, and a cordwainer—a maker of
shoes and other leather goods. "My father was
an honest man," John Adams would later recall,

"... and an independent spirit. ..."[1] Adams would remember his dear mother as "honored and beloved."[2]

Braintree Boyhood

As a boy, Adams greatly enjoyed growing up in Braintree. "I spent my time," he later recalled, "as idle Children do in making and sailing boats and Ships upon the Ponds and Brooks, in making and flying Kites ... playing marbles. ... Wrestling, Swimming, Skating and above all Shooting ..."[3] On many afternoons, he hiked the woods, hunting for squirrels and rabbits.

Adams's parents saw that he got an education. "I was very early taught to read at home," he remembered, "and at a School of Mrs. Belcher ... who lived ... on the opposite side of the Road."[4] When he grew older, Adams attended the local Latin School. It was a one-room school taught by Joseph Cleverly. One of Adams's classmates was young John Hancock.

In the crowded classroom, Mr. Cleverly paid little attention to Adams. The boy soon became bored with school, and he told his father so.

"What would you do, child?" his father asked.

"Be a farmer," the boy revealed.

"Well, I will show you what it is to be a farmer," his father told him.

John Adams was born in Braintree, Massachusetts, in the house pictured on the left. Adams inherited the house on the right, when his father died in 1761.

Throughout the next day, father and son sweated side by side, cutting marsh reeds for roof thatch. At the end of the long day, his father asked him how he liked being a farmer.

"I like it very well, sir," John answered.

"Ay, but I don't like it so well," his father told him. "So you shall go to school."[5]

John began attending Joseph Marsh's private school in Braintree, and he discovered he liked it.

Harvard Student

Because John was the oldest Adams son, it was decided that he would be the one to continue his studies. He would attend Harvard College in Cambridge, Massachusetts. Fifteen-year-old

John passed the entrance exam and was admitted in August 1751. His father sold ten acres of land to help pay the costs.

In 1751, Harvard consisted of four brick buildings, a small chapel, seven professors, and about one hundred students. "All scholars," the college rules demanded, were to "behave themselves blamelessly, leading sober, righteous, and godly lives."[6] As a freshman, Adams studied Greek, Latin, philosophy, and physics.

He worked hard and did well at Harvard. As his Harvard years progressed, he discovered he had "a growing Curiosity, a Love of Books and a fondness for Study . . ."[7] During his last two years of college, Adams joined a reading and debate club. During debates, Adams spoke with such skill and energy that his friends suggested he become a lawyer.

Worcester Schoolmaster

In July 1755, Adams graduated from Harvard near the top of his class. To earn enough money to study law, Adams obtained a position as a schoolmaster at Worcester, Massachusetts. The young Harvard graduate rode horseback sixty miles from Braintree west to Worcester in a single day. The next day, he began his teaching duties in Worcester's one-room schoolhouse. The fifty boys who jammed the classroom ranged in age from five to fifteen.

Adams was an ambitious young man. He yearned to do great things in his life. But sometimes he felt very gloomy about his future. In his diary, he wrote, "I have no Books, no Time, no Friends. I must therefore be contented to live and die an ignorant, obscure [unknown] fellow."[8]

In Worcester, Adams became a friend of James Putnam, a lawyer. When the colonial court was in session at Worcester, Putnam took Adams along to watch. Then, on August 22, 1756, Adams wrote in his diary: "Yesterday I completed a contract with Mr. Putnam to study law, under his inspection, for two years."[9] Putnam charged Adams a fee of one hundred dollars, and Adams moved into Putnam's house. Each day he taught at the Worcester schoolhouse, and each evening he read Putnam's law books.

When he completed his studies in October 1758, Adams quit teaching and returned home to Braintree. "I am beginning life anew," he happily told a Harvard classmate.[10] He often attended court in Boston where he respectfully listened to the city's leading lawyers present their cases. On November 6, 1759, Adams himself was formally welcomed as a lawyer. Within weeks, at age twenty-four, wearing the black gown and white wig of a lawyer, he took part in his first case.

A Budding Romance

In the summer of 1759, Adams went with a friend to Weymouth, Massachusetts. There he met Abigail Smith and her sisters, Mary and Elizabeth. They were the daughters of Reverend William Smith. Abigail Smith was fifteen years of age. She stood about five feet tall and had dark brown hair, bright brown eyes, and smooth, pale skin. Adams soon fell in love with her.

During their courtship, Adams often trotted his horse the five miles south to Weymouth. He found Abigail always cheerful and quick-witted. She was never afraid to speak her mind. He called her "Miss Adorable."[11]

On May 25, 1761, Adams's father died of influenza. Suddenly John became head of the Adams family. In his father's will, he was given the house next door to his mother's, as well as forty acres of land. He did farm work and established a law office in his house. As his law practice improved, he began riding the eight miles to Boston once or twice a week. In those days, there were not enough judges for every town. Judges followed a schedule and rode from town to town to hold court. It was called the legal circuit. Lawyers followed along, looking for work. Soon Adams was riding the legal circuit throughout Massachusetts colony. "I grow more expert . . . I feel my own strength," he admitted as his confidence grew.[12]

Married Life

On October 25, 1764, after a courtship of nearly five years, twenty-eight-year-old John Adams finally married nineteen-year-old Abigail Smith. They exchanged vows in a simple wedding ceremony in Weymouth. Her father conducted the ceremony. Immediately, the newlyweds moved into Adams's house in Braintree. Throughout their life together, Adams would always regard Abigail as his beloved equal.

On the Braintree farm, Abigail rose at dawn each day. She scattered feed for the ducks and chickens. She churned butter, baked, sewed, and worked hard on the farm. Adams continued his law career, going to Boston several times a week. But he declared, "I had rather chop wood, dig Ditches, and make a fence upon my poor little farm."[13] The couple's first child, Abigail, nicknamed Nabby, was born on July 14, 1765.

As a young lawyer, John Adams traveled throughout Massachusetts. But he preferred life on his farm in Braintree.

The Stamp Act

Massachusetts had been a British colony ever since Puritan settlers had landed at Plymouth Rock in 1620. Twelve other British colonies were established all along the Atlantic coast of North America. The people of these growing colonies owed their loyalty to Great Britain. Great Britain's royal government, called Parliament, appointed governors and other officials to rule the colonies. The colonists elected their own governing assemblies. But Great Britain sometimes passed new laws, which the colonists were required to obey. In the 1760s, Massachusetts lawyer James Otis sometimes spoke out against this policy. Otis believed free people deserved the right to take part in all aspects of their government. John Adams was greatly impressed with Otis and his speeches on self-government.

In the spring of 1765, news of a new British law reached the Massachusetts colony. It was called the Stamp Act. The Stamp Act taxed almost everything written or printed on paper, except for private letters and books. Pamphlets, newspapers, advertisements, deeds, college diplomas, and even playing cards were taxed. The British government had passed the Stamp Act to help pay the cost of the French and Indian War, which had occurred from 1754 to 1763. The French and Indian War had been fought to protect the colonists.

Therefore, the British government believed the colonists should pay a large part of its cost.

Throughout the thirteen American colonies, people were outraged by the Stamp Act. They did not want to pay the tax. The colonists were most upset because they had never been allowed a voice or vote on this issue. Americans had no elected members to speak for them in Parliament. Samuel Adams, an older second cousin of John Adams, formed a group called the Sons of Liberty. This group openly protested the tax in the streets of Boston. In August 1765, a mob of angry protesters stoned the homes of Andrew Oliver, secretary of the Massachusetts colony, and Lieutenant Governor Thomas Hutchinson. Both men were loyal representatives of King George III.

John Adams protested the Stamp Act, too, but in a more peaceful manner. He penned a newspaper article later entitled "The

Samuel Adams, a second cousin of John Adams, organized a revolutionary group of citizens called the Sons of Liberty.

True Sentiments of America." In it, he declared that American freedoms had been earned by the brave sacrifices of America's settlers. "Be it remembered," he declared, "that liberty must at all hazards [costs] be supported. We have a right to it."[14] When the article appeared in the *Boston Gazette*, it won the praise of many Massachusetts colonists.

Soon afterwards, Adams also wrote "The Braintree Instructions." This letter contained instructions from Braintree's citizens to their delegate in the Massachusetts General Court. The Massachusetts General Court could make laws for the colony. But laws received from Great Britain always had to be obeyed. "No freeman should be subject to any tax," Adams wrote in the letter, "to which he has not given his own consent." There must be "no taxation without representation."[15]

Quickly, forty other Massachusetts towns gave the same instructions to their delegates. This amounted to a formal protest demanding a voice in Parliament. "The Year 1765 has been the most remarkable Year of my Life," Adams wrote in his diary that December. "[T]he Stamp Act . . . has raised and spread thro the whole Continent, a Spirit that will be recorded to our Honor, with all future Generations."[16]

Successful Lawyer

The British government did away with the Stamp Act in the spring of 1766. In July 1767, Abigail Adams gave birth to a second baby, John Quincy. During this time, Adams attended to his law career, traveling to courts throughout the Massachusetts colony. He handled every kind of case, including murders. He often drew up deeds and other legal papers for clients. In 1768, he established a law office in Boston.

In 1767, the British government passed a new set of laws called the Townshend Acts. These laws taxed a variety of goods imported by the colonists from Great Britain. They included such items as glass, paint, lead, cloth, tea, and wine. Massachusetts colonists who resented these taxes sometimes tried to smuggle ship cargo into Boston without paying. John Hancock, Adams's boyhood schoolmate, was arrested in 1768 as a smuggler of wine. In court, Adams skillfully defended Hancock, who was found not guilty. The trial won Adams greater attention among Boston citizens.

For pleasure, Adams loved reading. He purchased books to fill the shelves of his Braintree home. "I want to see my wife and children every day," he once wrote, while away from home. "I want to see my grass and blossoms and corn. . . . But above all, except the wife and children, I want to see my books."[17] John Adams and his wife mourned the death of a baby daughter, Susanna, in February 1770. Soon after, an event occurred that made Adams famous throughout America.

The Boston Massacre

Throughout the colonies, people protested paying the taxes required by the Townshend Acts. Many colonists refused to wear clothes made from British cloth. Some colonists refused to drink tea. King George III and the British government believed that Boston troublemakers were causing most of the protests. It was decided that an example must be made in Boston. It would be a warning to all the colonies.

In 1768, warships landed regiments of British soldiers in Boston. They had come to enforce British law and remind Massachusetts citizens of the power of the king. The uniforms of the British soldiers included long red coats. As a result, they were nicknamed Redcoats.

Many Bostonians resented the presence of the Redcoats. Sometimes violence broke out between angry citizens and the British soldiers. On the cold evening of March 5, 1770, a foot of snow covered the Boston streets. A teenage boy began throwing snowballs at a soldier on guard duty in front of the customhouse. The customhouse was the place where tax on ship cargo was collected. Angry at being hit with snowballs, the soldier roughly grabbed the boy. The boy screamed out for help.

A crowd soon gathered, and the soldier nervously shouted for assistance. Seven soldiers hurried to the scene, commanded by Captain Thomas Preston. With loaded muskets and fixed bayonets, the soldiers faced the growing mob. Shouting curses and threats, the mob pelted the Redcoats with snowballs and chunks of ice. Then in a frightful instant, gunshots suddenly rang out. The soldiers had fired their muskets into the mob. Five men dropped to the ground, clutching deadly wounds: Crispus Attucks, Samuel Maverick, Samuel Gray, James Caldwell, and Patrick Carr. When they learned the news, shocked colonists called the killings the Boston Massacre.

Adams for the Defense

The day after the Boston Massacre, thirty-four-year-old John Adams was asked to defend the British soldiers. No one else, he was told, would take the case. Adams agreed, even though he realized it would put his entire law career in danger. Many Bostonians cursed the British soldiers as murderers. By defending them, it seemed to some people that Adams was supporting the military presence in the city. Still, Adams decided to risk his reputation and friendships by defending the soldiers. In the days that followed, angry Bostonians threw rocks through the windows of the Adamses' Boston home. But Adams remained unshakable. He believed that the British soldiers were innocent of any crime. He also claimed that, innocent or guilty, the soldiers deserved a fair trial. Gravely Adams predicted that this would be "as important a cause as had ever been tried in any court or country of the world."[18]

Captain Preston's trial was first. It began October 24, 1770, at Boston's new courthouse on Queen Street. In the crowded courtroom, Adams insisted that the soldiers had been threatened by the mob. He insisted that their lives had been in danger. Skillfully, he developed the facts. It could not be proved that Captain Preston had given an order to fire, as was charged. Thanks to Adams's arguments, the British officer was found not guilty.

At the second trial, the trial of the enlisted soldiers, Adams described the situation the night of the massacre: "the people crying, 'Kill them! Kill them! Knock them over!' heaving snowballs, oyster shells, clubs, white birch sticks. . . ."[19] He asked the jury to understand. Anyone in that situation would have feared that the mob was going to kill him. The tragedy, Adams's declared,

This sketch of the Boston Massacre shows British soldiers firing into a threatening mob on the night of March 5, 1770.

was the fault of the mob, not the soldiers. "Facts are stubborn things," he explained, "and whatever may be our wishes . . . they cannot alter the state of facts and evidence."[20] The jury spent two and a half hours before reaching its verdict. Of the eight soldiers, six were found not guilty. The other two were convicted of manslaughter. They had killed without planning the murder beforehand. The two were to be punished by having brands burned on their thumbs.

Adams later claimed that the Boston Massacre trials had cost him more than half his law business. But, he insisted, his defense of the British soldiers was "one of the most gallant, manly . . . actions of my whole life, and one of the best pieces of service I ever rendered my country."[21] The trial had proved that justice could triumph in Massachusetts. In time, Adams's reputation for honesty and fairness made him more respected than ever. He was even elected a Boston representative to the Massachusetts legislature in 1770. A second son, Charles, was born into the Adams family that year, and a third son, Thomas, was born in September 1772. "I [no longer take part in] public affairs," Adams noted, "and now have nothing to do but to mind my office, my clerks, and my children."[22] In May 1773, he decided to move his family back to the comforts of Braintree, keeping only an office in Boston.

The Boston Tea Party

The British law taxing tea imported by the thirteen colonies had been in force since 1767. In 1773, the British East India Company gained the exclusive right to sell tea. Upset colonists worried that their economy would be ruined by such a monopoly—a business that had no competition.

To protest a tax on tea, Boston citizens raided three ships in Boston Harbor, dumping cargoes of tea overboard. This incident became known as the Boston Tea Party.

Once again, they had had no voice in the British government's decision.

Samuel Adams and his Sons of Liberty were among the angriest of the colonists. On the night of December 16, 1773, dozens of protesters disguised as American Indians boarded three British cargo ships anchored in Boston Harbor. They dumped 342 chests of tea into the water. This protest became known as the Boston Tea Party. "Last Night, 3 Cargoes of Bohea Tea were emptied

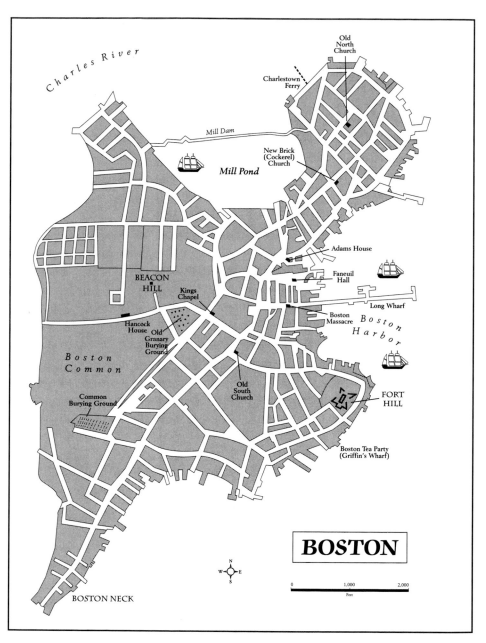

This map displays Boston, Massachusetts, during the time that John Adams lived there. Noted are the key locations of the Boston Massacre, the Boston Tea Party, and home of Adams.

into the Sea," Adams soon scribbled in his diary. "This is the most magnificent Movement of all."[23]

The British government harshly responded to the Boston Tea Party. In 1774, seven regiments of soldiers landed in Boston. The city became occupied territory. The British government also passed new laws that the colonists called the Intolerable Acts. These laws closed Boston Harbor and appointed a military governor for Massachusetts. All thirteen colonies now clearly understood the result of defying unfair British laws. "We live my dear soul, in an age of trial," Adams told Abigail.[24]

A Patriot in Congress

ON JUNE 17, 1774, the Massachusetts legislature picked John Adams to speak for the colony. He would be one of five delegates it was sending to a Continental Congress at Philadelphia. The Congress would meet in September to discuss the troubles between the colonies and Great Britain. Adams was flattered to be chosen, but he also felt humble. He stated, "I feel myself unequal to this Business."[1]

On August 10, 1774, Adams set out from Massachusetts by stagecoach with three of his fellow delegates. In the towns along the route, excited people cheered beside the road. Church bells rang out, and sometimes cannons boomed. "No governor of a province or general of an army," Adams exclaimed, "was ever treated with so much ceremony and assiduity [attention]."[2]

The First Continental Congress

On September 5, 1774, the First Continental Congress met in Philadelphia at Carpenter's Hall. It included fifty-six delegates from twelve colonies. Only Georgia was not represented. These gathered gentlemen impressed Adams. They represented the wisest and best educated men in the colonies. He wrote home, "There is in the Congress a collection of the greatest men upon this continent in point of abilities, virtues, and fortunes."[3]

In his opening speech, Virginia delegate Patrick Henry declared, "The [differences] between Virginians, Pennsylvanians, New Yorkers, and New Englanders, are no more. I am not a Virginian, but an American."[4] People in all of the colonies realized the danger of the Intolerable Acts. The British soldiers in Massachusetts could easily march into any other colony. United in purpose, the delegates agreed to a plan to boycott British goods in protest.

Lexington and Concord

The First Continental Congress ended on October 26, 1774. On his journey home, Adams noticed

Abigail Speaks Out

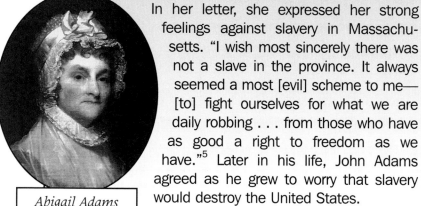

During the First Continental Congress, Abigail Adams wrote to her husband from Braintree. In her letter, she expressed her strong feelings against slavery in Massachusetts. "I wish most sincerely there was not a slave in the province. It always seemed a most [evil] scheme to me—[to] fight ourselves for what we are daily robbing . . . from those who have as good a right to freedom as we have."[5] Later in his life, John Adams agreed as he grew to worry that slavery would destroy the United States.

Abigail Adams

the spirit of liberty had truly taken root among New Englanders. With muskets on their shoulders, young men were drilling on village greens.

The American Revolution began in Massachusetts on April 19, 1775. Local militiamen clashed with British troops in the towns of Lexington and Concord. After the bloody fight, Adams rode to the scene and saw burned-out houses and women mourning for dead husbands and sons. Adams knew what war meant now. He understood that loyalty to Great Britain's King George III had ended for many Americans.

It was agreed that the Second Continental Congress would meet in May 1775. Once again

Adams was chosen as a delegate. He left his wife and small children behind in Braintree and journeyed back to Philadelphia.

The Second Continental Congress

Among the delegates to the Second Continental Congress was sixty-nine-year-old Benjamin Franklin. Franklin was America's most famous citizen. He was the witty writer of *Poor Richard's Almanac* and the inventor of the lightning rod.

Adams again found himself among delegates of uncommon talent and reputation. They included such fine men as George Washington of Virginia. "This assembly is like no other that ever existed," Adams wrote to Abigail. "Every man in it is a great man—an orator, a critic, a statesman. . . ."[6] John

On April 19, 1775, colonial militiamen clashed with British soldiers at Lexington, Massachusetts, in the first battle of the Revolutionary War.

Hancock of Massachusetts was elected to serve as president of the Congress. This was the same John Hancock who had been Adams's classmate as a boy and whom Adams had defended for smuggling in 1768.

The Congress's most urgent problem was to provide a commander in chief for the colonial militia gathering outside Boston. Adams insisted that wavering delegates be forced "to declare themselves for or against *something*." He told his cousin, Samuel Adams, "I am determined this morning to make a direct motion that Congress should adopt the army before Boston, and appoint Colonel Washington commander of it."[7]

True to his word, Adams obtained the floor and discussed the issue. He described Washington's high qualifications. The embarrassed Washington hurriedly left the room. Finally, Adams made his motion, and the vote was unanimous. Everyone had agreed. Soon after, Adams wrote to his wife, "I can now inform you that the Congress have made choice of . . . brave George Washington . . . to be general of the American army. . . . The liberties of America depend upon him in a great degree."[8]

The Work of Congress

The Continental Congress moved from Carpenters' Hall to the larger Pennsylvania State House.

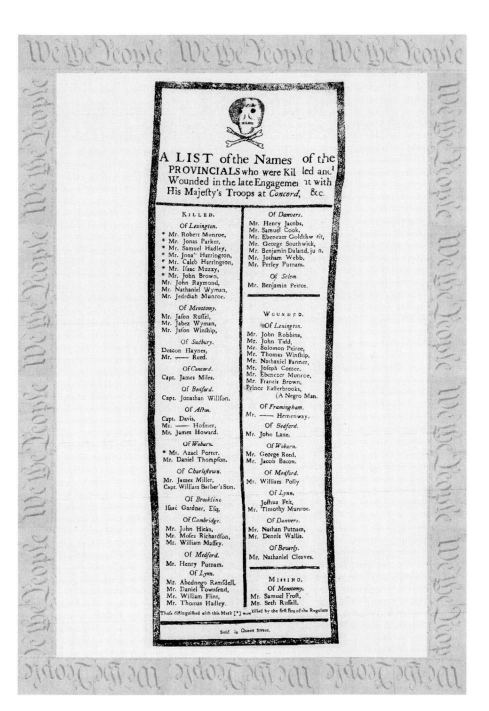

After the battles at Lexington and Concord, a notice was printed announcing the names of the militiamen killed or wounded.

Each day the delegates gathered there in the Assembly Room on the first floor. It was there that they learned of the Battle of Bunker Hill in Charleston, Massachusetts. On June 17, 1775, regiments of British Redcoats charged up the hill three times with heavy losses before the defending Americans were forced to retreat. In Braintree, Abigail took her seven-year-old son, John Quincy, to the top of Penn's Hill. Together they watched the distant smoke of the battle. "How many have fallen we know not," she wrote that night. "The constant roar of the cannon is so distressing that we cannot eat, drink, or sleep."[9]

Through the steaming summer heat of 1775, the Continental Congress met each day behind closed doors. From the start, Adams's honesty, intelligence, and energy won him the respect of his fellow delegates. They knew he had a quick temper. Still they chose him to serve on many of the Continental Congress's most important committees. He served, for example, on the Committee on Foreign Correspondence. The work of that committee was to obtain foreign aid. Adams described his daily routine: "I am really engaged in constant business from seven to ten in the morning in committee, from ten to four in Congress, and from six to ten again in committee."[10] He worked to the point of physical exhaustion. Nearly every day he joined in the

CHARLES TOWN

BOSTON

During the Battle of Bunker Hill, British troops captured the hill in Charleston, Massachusetts, at a bloody cost.

debates. The Continental Congress had many decisions to make. How was it to raise money to run the government? How were the colonies to deal with one another in business affairs? How should the American Indians on the frontier be treated? These and many other issues confronted the delegates.

One of Adams's chief concerns was building a navy. In October, the Continental Congress finally ordered that four swift warships would be constructed. The Continental Congress also voted that a Continental Army of 20,000 men would be raised.

Continued Debates

After a winter break, Adams returned to Philadelphia in February 1776. He now felt certain that fighting for independence was the only way Americans could protect their liberty.[11] The only question in his mind was when to make the declaration. Many delegates in Congress were still against such an extreme move. The idea might be voted down. Meanwhile, Adams joined in the daily debates, forcefully presenting his opinions. "Every important step was opposed, and carried by bare majorities," he later recalled, "which obliged [required] me to be almost

Common Sense

In January 1776, a revolutionary English immigrant named Thomas Paine published a pamphlet called *Common Sense*. It boldly called for American independence. "Why is it that we hesitate? . . . The sun never shined on a cause of greater worth . . . for God's sake, let us come to a final separation. . . . The birthday of a new world is at hand."[12] People snatched up *Common Sense*, and it sold 120,000 copies in just three months. Adams thought it was so important that he sent a copy to Abigail.

Thomas Paine

constantly engaged in debate. But I was not content with all that was done, and almost every day, I had something to say . . ."[13]

On March 4, 1776, General Washington's troops occupied the heights of Dorchester overlooking Boston. The next day, the roar of American cannons rattled the windows of the Adams home in Braintree. British General William Howe soon realized he could no longer defend Boston. On March 17, 1776, Abigail Adams again climbed to the top of Penn's Hill. She stared in amazement at the sight of the British abandoning Boston. Within days, the entire British fleet had steered out to sea. "You may count upwards of one hundred and seventy-sail," she declared in a letter. "They look like a forest."[14]

A Resolution for Independence

In the spring of 1776, Adams wrote an essay. He called it "Thoughts on Government." The essay outlined Adams's ideas on how state governments should be run. Adams believed the best design for a government was one in which there were executive, legislative, and judicial branches. Adams proposed that the legislative branch be made up of two elected chambers (house and senate). The legislative branch would make state laws. The executive branch (the governor) would enforce the laws. The judicial branch (the court system) would interpret the laws. In this manner, no single branch of government would have too much power. Each branch could hold in check the actions of the others. This system of "checks and balances" would be the kind of government the Constitutional Convention of 1787 would design for the United States.

While Adams penned his essay, the Second Continental Congress slowly edged closer to declaring independence. That spring, the delegates of three southern colonies, South Carolina, Georgia, and North Carolina, received instructions allowing them to vote for independence. It seemed there was growing agreement that independence must come.

"What in the name of Common Sense are you gentlemen of the Continental Congress about? Is it dozing?" wrote one impatient

George Washington took command of the Continental Army in 1775. In March 1776, his troops forced the British to abandon Boston.

I long to hear that you have declared an independency. . . . And, by the way, in the new code of laws which I suppose it will be necessary for you to make, I desire you would remember the ladies and be more generous and favorable to them than your ancestors. Do not put unlimited power into the hands of the husbands. Remember, all men would be tyrants if they could.[15]

Two weeks after the British left Boston in March 1776, Abigail Adams wrote a letter to her husband. In her letter, she advised him to acknowledge American women within the new political system.

Massachusetts citizen to Adams. "The only question is concerning the proper time for making a specific declaration in words," Adams responded, "But remember you can't make thirteen clocks strike precisely [exactly] alike at the same second."[16]

The moment that Adams had worked so hard to achieve finally arrived on June 7, 1776. That day, delegate Richard Henry Lee of Virginia rose in Congress. He formally made a motion that "these United Colonies are, and of right ought to be, free and independent states."[17] It was John Adams who immediately seconded the historic motion.

Writing a Declaration

Delegates against independence managed to delay the final vote until July 1. This allowed some delegates enough time to send to their colonies for new instructions. But Congress agreed that a declaration of independence should be prepared in the meantime. A committee was appointed consisting of John Adams, Roger Sherman, Robert Livingston, Benjamin Franklin, and Virginia delegate Thomas Jefferson.

John Adams and Thomas Jefferson were very different in appearance. Adams was short, stout, and balding. Jefferson was tall and lean. His hair was a fiery red in color. Adams was never afraid to speak out and give his opinion on matters. Jefferson rarely spoke in Congress. "During the whole Time I sat with him in Congress," Adams later remarked, "I never heard him utter three sentences together."[18]

Adams was from the North, and Jefferson was from the South. Yet the two men had much in common. They both loved study, books, and the beauty of words. More importantly, both men were determined to win independence for America. Years later, in 1812, delegate Benjamin Rush declared to Adams, "I consider you and [Jefferson] as the North and South Poles of the American Revolution. Some talked, some wrote, and some fought to promote and establish it, but you and Jefferson thought for us all."[19] Adams had a high opinion of Jefferson's mind, and Jefferson later commented, "Mr. A. [Adams] and myself were cordial friends from the beginning of the revolution."[20]

When it came time to write a declaration of independence, Jefferson suggested that Adams write the important document. But Adams insisted Jefferson was the one to do it.

"Why?" Jefferson asked.

"Reasons enough," Adams answered.

"What can be your reasons?"

"Reason first: you are a Virginian and a Virginian ought to appear at the head of this business. [Virginia was the largest colony.] Reason second: I am obnoxious, suspected and unpopular. You are very much otherwise. Reason third: You can write ten times better than I can."[21]

In his boardinghouse room at Seventh and Market streets, Jefferson took up his pen and went to work.

> $\boldsymbol{\mathcal{W}}$*e hold these truths to be self-evident, that all men are created equal, that they are endowed by their Creator with certain unalienable Rights, that among these are Life, Liberty, and the pursuit of Happiness.—That to secure these rights, Governments are instituted among Men, deriving their just powers from the consent of the governed . . .*[22]

In the Declaration of Independence, Thomas Jefferson wrote stirring words that many Americans know by heart. Today, this important document is kept where visitors can see it at the National Archives in Washington, D.C.

Dark Days of War

On July 1, 1776, John Adams battled with Pennsylvania delegate John Dickinson in the final debate on independence. The next day, July 2, twelve of the thirteen delegations voted for independence from Great Britain. New York abstained from voting that day but would vote for independence later.

Before the end of July, Adams was serving on twenty-five committees in Congress. His fellow delegates also chose him to serve as president of Congress's new Continental Board of War and Ordnance. This position made him responsible for obtaining weapons and building forts, raising troops, and providing military supplies for the Continental Army. Adams understood General Washington's dangerous situation well.

In August 1776, 15,000 British and hired Hessian soldiers commanded by General William Howe landed on Long Island, New York. General Washington's poorly equipped army gathered to face them. The American force numbered only 8,000. Washington's soldiers were soon defeated near Brooklyn Heights. The beaten Continental troops fled to Manhattan Island. Adams vowed in a letter to Abigail, "The panic may seize whom it will, it will not seize me."[23] Adams's unshakable spirit inspired other members of Congress. Delegate Benjamin Rush declared of Adams, "This illustrious [brilliant] patriot has not his superior, scarcely his equal for abilities and virtue on the whole of the continent of America."[24]

Further defeats in New York—at White Plains and Fort Washington—forced Washington to retreat across New Jersey into Pennsylvania in December. Philadelphia was threatened with invasion. The Congress fled south to Baltimore,

Here, the committee assigned to draft the Declaration of Independence presents the document to Congress. John Adams stands at the center with his hand on his hip. Seated across from him is John Hancock.

Maryland. The dream of American freedom looked very dark indeed.

Then suddenly, on Christmas night 1776, Washington and his troops crossed the Delaware River. They made a successful surprise attack on the Hessian garrison at Trenton, New Jersey. Washington's soldiers stung the enemy again on January 2, 1777, when they attacked the British at Princeton, New Jersey. Adams returned with the Congress to Philadelphia in the spring of 1777. Between his work as a delegate and his duty on the military board, he scarcely had time to sleep. "This Day compleats Six Months since I left you," he wrote to Abigail that summer. "I am wasted and exhausted in Mind and Body. . . ."[25]

In August 1777, British warships landed Howe's British army south of Philadelphia. The Redcoat troops prepared to march into the city. Washington's army failed to slow the advancing enemy in a fierce fight on September 11 at Brandywine Creek. On September 26, Howe's invading troops entered the streets of Philadelphia.

General Washington led a charge into Trenton, New Jersey, on December 26, 1776. The Hessian troops stationed in that city were caught by surprise.

Adams and the rest of the Congress had already fled to York, Pennsylvania. It had been a season of disaster for the Americans. But Adams had reason to be hopeful. News arrived that British General John Burgoyne had been defeated at the Battle of Saratoga in New York on October 17. Burgoyne had surrendered his entire army of 5,000 men to an American force commanded by General Horatio Gates. The Battle of Saratoga marked a turning point in the American Revolution.

Foreign Diplomat

IN NOVEMBER 1777, forty-two-year-old John Adams took leave of Congress and returned home to Massachusetts. He hardly had time to rest. On December 15, he learned Congress had named him as a commissioner to France. As a diplomat, Adams would try to arrange a French alliance with the United States.

Commissioner to France

Since March 1777, American commissioners Benjamin Franklin, Arthur Lee, and Silas Deane had been in France. Adams had been chosen to replace Deane. Abigail decided to remain at home to run the farm. But ten-year-old John

Quincy would travel with his father. It would be a risky journey. Adams knew that the British would probably put him on trial for treason if he were captured. But his sense of duty, ambition, and patriotism drew him onward.

On February 13, 1778, father and son set sail aboard the ship *Boston*. During the ocean voyage, a British warship tried to capture the *Boston*. Adams urged the crew to fight if necessary. "It would have been more eligible for me to be killed on board the *Boston* or sunk to the bottom in her than to be taken Prisoner," Adams concluded afterward.[1] However, the *Boston* escaped capture. After five weeks at sea, the ship finally reached the coast of France. When he reached Paris, Adams learned that the American victory at Saratoga already had persuaded France to sign an alliance with the United States. His main reason for coming to France already had been accomplished.

On May 8, 1778, Adams was presented to King Louis XVI. At first, the French thought the stout American was the famous Samuel Adams. Adams explained that the founder of the Sons of Liberty was his cousin. Always critical of himself, Adams afterwards made a note in his diary. The French, he wrote, had decided he was "a man of whom nobody had ever heard before . . . a man who did not understand a word of

Benjamin Franklin in Paris

Benjamin Franklin made a tremendous impression upon the French people. Before his arrival in 1777, they already admired him for his scientific experiments. Wherever he appeared, French crowds cheered him. Fashionable ladies took to wearing bearskin hats like the one he wore. His face appeared in pictures, on medals, and even painted on the lids of snuffboxes. Franklin used his popularity to good advantage when negotiating with the French on behalf of the United States.

Benjamin Franklin

French; awkward in his figure, awkward in his dress; no abilities. . . ."[2]

Thankless Work

Adams soon discovered commissioners Benjamin Franklin and Arthur Lee did not like one another. On August 7, 1778, he wrote, "I am between two gentlemen of opposite tempers. . . . Yet both may be and I believe are honest men, and devoted friends to their country."[3] While Franklin and Lee feuded, Adams took upon himself most of the work of the commission. He wrote letters, balanced the financial accounts, and arranged passports for American travelers. He also searched the London newspapers and magazines for news he could send to Congress. "I found that the Business of our Commission would never be done, unless I did it," he declared.[4]

Adams discovered that he and Franklin had very different diplomatic styles. He respected Franklin as a true patriot. But he felt Franklin was too relaxed, almost lazy, in dealing with the French. Franklin enjoyed going to dinners and parties. He liked flirting with French noblewomen during visits to their homes. Franklin's life in France appeared to Adams to be "an endless round of social events."[5] Adams failed to realize how much Franklin could accomplish with gentle coaxing. Over time, Franklin greatly influenced the French government's policy toward the United States.

Compared to Franklin, Adams seemed very pushy. Adams wanted immediate action from the French. He bombarded the Count de Vergennes, the French foreign minister, with letters. The letters bluntly urged that French armies, warships, and supplies quickly be sent to aid the United States. The French government was not willing to make such hasty decisions. In time, the Count de Vergennes grew to resent Adams's constant impatience. Benjamin Franklin later commented that Adams was "Always an honest man, often a wise one, but sometimes, and in some things, absolutely out of his senses."[6]

On February 12, 1779, news arrived that Congress had named Benjamin Franklin as the only minister (ambassador) to France. Adams's duties as a commissioner had come to an end. He had no instructions, and he complained that "Congress had not taken the least notice" of him; "they never so much as bid me come home, bid me stay, or told me I had done well or done ill."[7] His feelings deeply hurt, he made arrangements to sail home to Massachusetts.

The Massachusetts Constitution

Adams and John Quincy reached Boston on August 2, 1779. Within days, the town of Braintree chose Adams as its representative at the state's constitutional convention. On September 1, Adams joined the delegates meeting in Cambridge, Massachusetts. Of the 250 delegates, it was Adams who was chosen to write the state's constitution.

By early October, Adams had drafted "A Constitution or Form of Government for the Commonwealth of Massachusetts." It guaranteed free elections, "freedom of speaking" and "liberty of the press."[8] It divided the state government into three branches—the legislative, the executive, and the judicial. Today, the constitution of the Commonwealth of Massachusetts is the oldest constitution still in use in the world.

Return to Europe

On September 27, 1779, Congress chose John Adams to return to France. As minister "plenipotentiary," Adams was given full power to arrange an American peace treaty with Great Britain. "Upon the whole I am of the opinion that in . . . Congress, your character is as high as any gentleman's in America," delegate Elbridge Gerry told him.[9]

Again Abigail would stay at home. But nine-year-old Charles and twelve-year-old John Quincy would both travel with their father. On November 15, they sailed from Boston aboard the *Sensible*. During the voyage, a storm badly damaged the ship. Anxiously the captain sailed for the nearest port at Ferrol, Spain. "We have had an escape again," Adams wrote to Abigail.[10] "One more storm would very probably [have] carried us to the bottom of the sea," young John Quincy exclaimed when he wrote home.[11] An overland journey of 1,200 miles at last brought them to Paris, France, on February 9, 1780.

Looking to the Dutch

While in Paris, Adams waited impatiently to be contacted by the British. Feeling useless in

France, Adams soon turned his attention to a nation to the north, the Netherlands. He hoped he could persuade the Dutch government to recognize the United States. He also hoped he could convince Dutch bankers to loan money to the United States. If he could arrange these two things, he knew he would greatly help the war effort. Adams removed his sons from the school, and on July 27, 1780, they journeyed north to the Hague, the Dutch capital.

Adams realized he needed to convince the Dutch that America could win independence. Otherwise, Dutch bankers would never risk loaning money. But the Dutch government did not even recognize that the United States existed. "Very few dare to see me," he reported.[12] In five months, Adams failed to meet a single government official of any importance.

In June 1781, Adams learned that Congress had named Benjamin Franklin, John Jay, Henry Laurens, and Thomas Jefferson to join him as peace commissioners to meet with representatives of Great Britain. Adams felt lonely as the summer of 1781 turned to fall. His homesick son Charles had sailed back to Massachusetts. John Quincy was traveling to Russia to become secretary to the American minister there. John Adams labored on alone when news arrived in the Netherlands that sent his heart soaring. On

October 19, 1781, at Yorktown, Virginia, British General Lord Charles Cornwallis had surrendered his army of 7,000 to an American and French force commanded by George Washington. Clearly the American victory at Yorktown signaled an end to the war.

On April 19, 1782, the Dutch government finally recognized the United States as an independent nation. Within weeks, Adams raised the American flag at "The United States House." It was the first American embassy anywhere in the

In this print, British General Lord Cornwallis surrenders at Yorktown, Virginia. The American victory at Yorktown in October 1781 was the last great battle of the American Revolution.

world. After months of toil, he had finally succeeded. "Nobody knows that I do anything; or have anything to do," he wrote. "One thing, thank God! is certain. I have planted the American standard [flag] at the Hague. There let it wave and fly in triumph over . . . British pride."[13] In June, Adams at last obtained a Dutch bank loan of $2 million for the United States. It was money greatly needed by Congress. The loan helped establish American credit throughout Europe.

The Treaty of Paris

In Paris, Benjamin Franklin and John Jay were already discussing peace with British commissioners. Thomas Jefferson was still in America, and Henry Laurens was delayed in London, England. On October 26, 1782, John Adams reached Paris. Congress had instructed the American commissioners to follow the advice of the French government in reaching terms of peace. Both Jay and Franklin agreed with Adams that this instruction should be ignored. Adams insisted, "It is a glory to have broken such infamous orders."[14]

Formal meetings with the British commissioners began on October 30, Adams's forty-seventh birthday. Richard Oswald was the chief negotiator for the British. The British were anxious for peace now. They quickly agreed to recognize American independence. But there were other important issues that needed to be decided. These issues included the boundaries of the United States, the right of navigation on the Mississippi River, and American fishing rights on the Grand Banks off Newfoundland.

Adams, Franklin, and Jay insisted that, in addition to the thirteen colonies, Britain give up all the territory from the Appalachian Mountains to the Mississippi River. The British agreed, doubling the size of the United States. America's right to use the Mississippi River was also soon settled. Then Adams took up the argument for America's fishing rights off Newfoundland. New England fishermen had been sailing there for years. "Gentlemen," Adams declared, "is there or can there be a clearer right? . . . If war, and blood, and treasure give a right, ours is as good as yours."[15]

The American and British commissioners finally agreed on every article. The Treaty of Paris was signed at the Hotel d'York on September 3, 1783. John Adams, Benjamin Franklin, and John Jay signed the historic document on behalf of the United States. The first sentence of Article I declared, "His Britannic Majesty acknowledges the said United States . . . to be free, sovereign and independent states."[16] After eight hard years of war, the American Revolution had ended.

Minister to Great Britain

"Oh when shall I see my dearest Friend," Adams wrote to Abigail.[17] With peace restored, Abigail finally agreed to join him in Europe. She and Nabby crossed the Atlantic Ocean in the summer of 1784. Soon they were settled with Adams and John Quincy in a rented mansion in Auteuil, a village outside Paris. While in France, Adams met daily with Benjamin Franklin and Thomas Jefferson. The three attempted to obtain business treaties with the various European nations. In the end, they were able to make only one treaty, with Prussia (part of Germany today).

On April 26, 1785, Adams opened a letter from Congress. It revealed that he had been named America's first minister to Great Britain. John Quincy soon sailed for home to attend Harvard College. Later that month, Adams, Abigail, and Nabby departed Auteuil for London, England. They moved into a house on Grosvenor Square. "It is a decent House," Nabby reported to John Quincy, "a little out of repairs, but such a one as you would not blush to see our Foreign Minister in."[18] Romance soon bloomed between Nabby Adams and Colonel William Smith, Adams's diplomatic secretary. In time, Adams and Abigail agreed to their daughter's marriage to Smith.

The Unwelcome Minister

On June 1, 1785, Minister Adams was presented to King George III. Adams formally bowed three times upon his entrance into the king's chamber. "The United States of America have appointed me their minister . . . to Your Majesty," Adams stated, nearly overcome by the importance of the moment.[19]

In the days following this interview, however, the Adams family found themselves ignored by British officials. King George III treated Adams with coldness, and nearly the whole court circle followed the king's example. Abigail described the atmosphere as "not the pleasantest in the world."[20]

The British seemed to believe that America's experiment in democracy would surely fail. Many British people regarded the arrival of a diplomat from the United States as little more than a joke. "An ambassador from America! Good heavens what a sound!" scoffed the *London Public Advertiser*.[21] Attacks on Adams in British newspapers became quite common. After reading some London newspapers that criticized Adams, Thomas Jefferson declared, "Indeed a man must be of rock who can stand all this."[22]

In May 1786, Adams returned to the Netherlands to obtain still another badly needed Dutch loan for the United States. He knew he had done his best as American minister to

Great Britain. But he had achieved little to help American relations with that country. He was fifty-two years of age. Except for his brief visit to Massachusetts in 1778, he had been away from the United States for ten long years. On April 20, 1788, he and Abigail set sail for home.

At Home in Braintree

Thousands of American colonists crowded the Boston waterfront when the ship *Lucretia* docked on June 17, 1788. They cheered the arrival of the old patriot John Adams.

King George III of Great Britain, bitter after the loss of the American colonies, treated John Adams with coldness.

Both Adams and Abigail were glad to finally reach Braintree. Adams declared he planned to "embrace it with both arms and all my might. There live, there to die, there to lay my bones. . . ."[23]

While in London, Adams had arranged to purchase the Braintree house and ninety-five acre farm of Major Leonard Vassall. The house needed repairs, but Adams was very pleased

He is not qualified by nature or education to shine in courts. . . . *He* cannot dance, drink, game, flatter, promise, dress, swear with the gentlemen, and [make] small talk and flirt with the ladies; in short, he has none of the essential arts or ornaments which constitute a courtier.[24]

In a letter, Jonathan Sewall, a Massachusetts friend living in London, commented on Adams's character as minister.

with it. "It is not large, in the first place," he admitted. "It is but the farm of a patriot."[25] Adams fondly called his new home "Peacefield." He had spent thirteen years of his life in the service of his country. Now he happily became a private citizen again.

First Vice President of the United States

GEORGE WASHINGTON WAS the clear choice to become the first president of the United States. Washington was from Virginia in the South. As a result, many people thought a New Englander from the North should be selected as vice president. John Adams's name was at the top of the list of candidates.

Choosing National Leaders

The new Constitution declared that the president was to be chosen by electors—people entitled to participate in an election. Some states decided to let their legislatures chose electors. In other states, electors were chosen by popular votes.

Each elector was to cast a ballot with the names of two choices for president. The candidate with the most votes would become president. The one with the second largest number would be named vice president.

When the election ballots were opened on February 4, 1789, they revealed that Washington had received a vote from every one of the sixty-nine electors. In second place with thirty-four votes was fifty-three-year-old John Adams—well ahead of ten other candidates! Adams learned he had been chosen the first vice president of the United States.

New York City was the temporary capital of the federal government. Adams left Boston on April 13, 1789. Forty carriages escorted him out of the city in a grand parade. In New York City on April 21, senators greeted Adams on the corner of Broad and Wall streets at the door of Federal Hall—the place where Congress met. They escorted him upstairs to the Senate Chamber. In an informal ceremony, Senator John Langdon of New Hampshire led Adams to the vice president's chair at the head of the chamber. In a brief speech, Adams declared he "cheerfully and readily" accepted the duties of vice president. "The eyes of the world are upon you," he told the assembled senators.[1] The new government would have many decisions to make.

Nine days later on April 30, 1789, George Washington was inaugurated at Federal Hall. Adams formally welcomed Washington and escorted him to the outer balcony. The street below was packed with spectators. People jammed the neighboring windows and crowded the rooftops to witness the historic event. Adams proudly watched as George Washington took the oath of office as first president of the United States.

The New Government

Adams rented a house called Richmond Hill, a mile north of the city. "Never," he wrote, "did I live in so delightful a spot."[2] Abigail traveled south and joined him there in June.

As vice president, Adams had two main duties, as described by the Constitution. The first duty was only necessary if the president died in office. Then the vice president would become president. The second duty, however, required that the vice president preside over, or run, the Senate when it was in session. "The Vice President of the United States," declared the Constitution, "shall be President of the Senate, but shall have no vote, unless they be equally divided."[3] The small Senate was almost equally divided on many important questions. Adams sometimes found himself casting the deciding vote.

In spring of 1789, twenty-two senators gathered each day at Federal Hall. (North Carolina and Rhode Island had not yet ratified the Constitution and therefore did not have senators.) Not all the senators liked Vice President Adams. "John Adams has neither judgment, firmness of mind, nor respectability of deportment [good manners] to fill the chair of such an assembly," Pennsylvania Senator William Maclay soon decided.[4] In spite of Maclay's opinion, Adams managed to establish dignity in the Senate. Sitting in his chair, he sharply rapped a silver pencil case on his table to maintain order.

One early issue discussed in the Senate concerned how the president should be officially addressed. Adams thought Washington should be given the title "His Majesty the President."[5] Senator Maclay sourly commented, "I think our Vice President may go and dream about titles, for none will he get."[6] In the end, Congress voted that Washington's title be simply "The President of the United States."

Adams's conservative views and sometimes abrupt manner bothered some of the senators. Some people muttered that Adams had returned from Great Britain a great admirer of kings and royalty. Adams gave them the impression that he favored monarchy instead of democracy. Behind his back, some senators mocked Adams's round, plump figure and called him "His Rotundity."[7] Adams denied that he favored monarchy. "If you suppose," he wrote in a letter to Thomas Jefferson, "that I have or ever had a . . . desire . . . to introduce a government of Kings . . . into . . . the United States . . . you are wholly mistaken."[8]

Through the sweltering summer of 1789, Adams attended the Senate every day. The Senate soon passed the Judiciary Act, which established a national court system.

In the Senate Chamber at Federal Hall (pictured), Vice President John Adams sat on the platform at the right.

Federalists and Republicans

President Washington chose Alexander Hamilton as secretary of the treasury, Thomas Jefferson as secretary of state, Edmund Randolph as attorney general, and Henry Knox as secretary of war. Alexander Hamilton was a New York businessman who favored a strong federal government. He supported the interests of the nation's merchants, bankers, and manufacturers. Jefferson, on the other hand, favored farmers. Jefferson feared the growing power of the federal government over the states. Both men worried that the other would destroy the government if given too much power.

In the summer of 1789, Americans learned a revolution had occurred in France. King Louis XVI was overthrown, and a radical democratic government established. Hamilton disliked and distrusted the new French government. Instead, he strongly favored better relations with Great Britain. Jefferson, however, believed the French Revolution would become another great leap for democracy, like the American Revolution. Hamilton's political supporters began calling themselves Federalists. Jefferson's political supporters took the name Republicans. (Jefferson's Republicans in time came to be called Republican-Democrats and today more simply Democrats.) "There is nothing I dread so much as a division of the Republic into two great [political] parties, each in opposition to each other," worried Adams.[9]

Through the winter of 1789, Congress battled over where to locate the permanent national capital. New Englanders preferred New York City. Pennsylvanians desired Philadelphia. Virginians wanted a new capital to be built in the South, on the Maryland side of the Potomac River. In exchange for a national banking system and other nationalist programs, Hamilton and the Federalists finally agreed to support the plan for the Potomac. Congress voted that Philadelphia be the temporary capital until 1800. Then the government would move south to the new federal District of Columbia.

Alexander Hamilton supported American business interests, a strong national government, and better relations with Great Britain.

In 1792, citizens in Braintree argued over the spending of the town's school funds. As a result, the people of North Braintree broke away. They established a new independent township called Quincy. Adams discovered his home was in Quincy now.

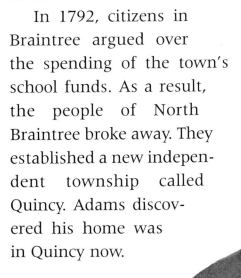

The Election of 1792

Throughout his four-year term as vice president, Adams had been loyal to President Washington. As Senate president, Adams had broken twenty tie votes, all favoring Washington's positions.

As the election of 1792 approached, most Americans agreed that Washington must serve a second term. "North and South will hang together if they have you to hang on," Thomas Jefferson told the president.[10] Citizens of the South generally supported Jefferson's Republican policies. This was because many Southerners were farmers. Citizens of the North most often supported Hamilton's Federalist ideals. In the North, there were growing numbers of merchants, businessmen, and manufacturers. Only Washington was respected enough to hold the young nation together. In November 1792, Washington announced that he would accept a second term.

Vermont and Kentucky had joined the union by 1792. Electors in the fifteen states cast their ballots. When the electoral votes were tallied in February 1793, the final count revealed: Washington 132 votes, Adams 77 votes, George Clinton 50, Thomas Jefferson 4, and Aaron Burr 1. John Adams had been chosen vice president for a second term to begin March 4, 1793.

Staying Neutral

Congress was only in session about six months each year. Adams remained in Quincy the rest of the time. Abigail, however, chose to stay at home the entire time, to protect her health and to run the farm.

In 1793, France and Great Britain went to war. In early April, "Citizen" Edmund Charles Genet, the new ambassador from France, arrived in the United States. Genet had been sent to America with instructions to win American support for France in its war with Britain. But on April 22, Washington issued a Proclamation of Neutrality. He refused to let the United States take sides and become an ally of France. Adams agreed completely with this neutrality policy. Fourteen years earlier, he had written from France, "Let us above all things avoid as much as possible entangling ourselves with their ways and politics."[11]

At times, Adams seemed bored with his duties as vice president. "I go to the Senate every day," he wrote Abigail, "read the newspapers before I go . . . see a few friends once a week, go to church on Sundays; write now and then a line to you. . . ."[12] He realized the vice presidency was not a powerful office. "My country in its wisdom contrived for me the most insignificant office that ever the invention of man contrived or

Yellow Fever

Yellow fever raged through Philadelphia in August 1793. During the deadly epidemic, the federal government and most businesses closed as people fled the city. It was believed that the stinking, hot city air caused yellow fever. (In 1900, Dr. Walter Reed proved that mosquitoes transmit yellow fever.) By October 1793, more than a hundred people were dying each day in Philadelphia. In all, more than 5,000 died in the epidemic. A second epidemic in 1798 would claim another 3,000 lives.

his imagination conceived."[13] Sitting silently in the Senate Chamber, Vice President Adams often yearned to take active part in the debates.

Family Pride

Thomas and Charles Adams had become lawyers. Nabby Adams Smith and her family had returned from England and had settled in upstate New York. It was John Quincy Adams, however, that gave his father the greatest joy. "All my hopes are in him," Adams declared, "both for my family and my country."[14]

John Quincy Adams had lived in the Netherlands. He knew the Dutch language and the country. It made good sense when, in May 1794, President Washington chose John Quincy to be minister to the Netherlands. John Quincy sailed for Europe in September 1794. He took his brother Thomas along to serve as his private secretary.

The Election of 1796

In its war with France, the British Navy needed sailors. In 1793, the British had begun stopping American ships and "impressing" sailors. The British claimed the sailors were British citizens and forced them to serve on British ships. Angry Americans demanded war against Great Britain. Instead, President Washington sent John Jay to bargain with the British. In June 1796, Congress agreed to the peace terms Jay arranged. The danger of war had passed. By that time, Adams had already returned home to Massachusetts. His term as vice president was nearly over. During his eight years in office, Adams had cast a total of thirty-one tie-breaking votes. No vice president in American history has ever cast more.

Adams and Thomas Jefferson were the leading candidates for president in

This portrait shows John Quincy Adams, John Adams's eldest son, who become minister to the Netherlands in 1794.

1796. Throughout the fall, Jefferson remained at his Virginia estate, Monticello. Adams remained at Peacefield. Neither took an active role in the political campaign. Back then, it was considered good manners for a presidential candidate to simply wait and be chosen for office.

The election of 1796 became one of the bitterest in United States history. Republican newspapers fiercely attacked Adams's reputation. The Philadelphia *Aurora*, for example, declared that Adams was unfit to lead the country. The newspaper called him the "champion of kings, ranks, and titles. . . ."[15] Adams's supporters in the Federalist party called Jefferson the "friend of France."[16] They mocked his religious beliefs and called him a coward. (Jefferson had fled Monticello when British cavalry raided in 1781 during the American Revolution.)

The Federalists decided on a plan to win electoral votes in the South. They named former minister to Spain Thomas Pinckney of South Carolina as Adams's running mate. To pick up Northern votes, the Republicans chose Senator Aaron Burr of New York to run with Jefferson. The voting for presidential electors occurred in November. On November 23, 1796, Adams said goodbye to Abigail and journeyed south to Philadelphia. It was Adams's official duty as vice president to open the electoral ballots. On

February 8, 1797, he officially announced the result of the vote: Adams 71, Jefferson 68, Pinckney 59, Burr 30, and Samuel Adams 11. By three votes, John Adams had been elected the president of the United States by the Federalists. Republican Thomas Jefferson, with the second highest number of votes, would be vice president.

Second President of the United States

ON INAUGURATION DAY, March 4, 1797, Adams arrived at Congress Hall in Philadelphia in a hansom carriage. At noon, members of the House and Senate, justices of the Supreme Court, Cabinet members, and foreign diplomats jammed the House Chamber. While George Washington looked on, sixty-one-year-old John Adams took the oath of office.

None of the Adams family was present at the inauguration. Adams wrote Abigail a letter afterward describing the event. Washington seemed "to enjoy a triumph over me," he revealed. "Methought I heard him say, 'Ay, I am fairly out and you fairly in! See which of us will be happiest!'"[1]

After years of faithful service to his country, John Adams (pictured) was elected to be the second president of the United States.

Early Decisions

One of Adams's first decisions as president was to ask Washington's Cabinet members to remain in office. "Washington had appointed them and I knew it would turn the world upside down if I removed any one of them," he later wrote.[2] So, Secretary of State Timothy Pickering, Secretary of the Treasury Oliver Wolcott, Secretary of War James McHenry, and Attorney General Charles Lee remained at the heads of their departments. Adams failed to realize Pickering, Wolcott, and McHenry were loyal followers of Alexander Hamilton. Hamilton hoped that his influence with them would allow him to control government policy. These men were all Federalists. George Washington had often supported Federalist policies. But Washington had never declared himself a member of a political party. The same was true of John Adams. Adams wished to be independent and not completely govern following Federalist political policies.

Before leaving office, Washington had written Adams a letter. "I give it as my decided opinion," Washington wrote, "Mr. [John Quincy] Adams is the most valuable public character we have abroad, and there remains no doubt in my mind that he will prove himself to be the ablest of all our diplomatic corps. . . ."[3] President Adams soon chose his able son to serve as America's minister to Prussia.

The Threat of War

In 1797, French warships seized American ships. President Adams soon faced the threat of open war. Federalist newspapers declared France the enemy of the United States. Republican editors countered with friendly opinions of the French. On May 15, 1797, Adams declared that he was ready "to [make] a fresh attempt at negotiation."[4] He would ask American and French diplomats to discuss the problem. But at the same time, he proposed building a strong navy to protect American shipping. He also recommended that the army be increased. Adams hoped to keep the nation out of war, but he could not allow France to trample on American honor. Within days, he appointed three peace commissioners to travel to Paris: General Charles Cotesworth Pinckney, John Marshall, and Elbridge Gerry. Adams needed good advice, and once again he turned to his wife. "The times are critical and dangerous and I must have you here to assist me," he told her. "I can do nothing without you."[5] Abigail left Quincy and hurried to his side in Philadelphia.

No Peace in Congress

In January 1798, a fight took place on the floor of the House of Representatives. It was the first physical assault ever to occur in Congress. In the midst of debate, Federalist Roger Griswold of Connecticut insulted Republican Matthew Lyon of Vermont. Lyon quickly responded by crossing the chamber and spitting in Griswold's face. Griswold then began swinging at Lyon with a cane. Lyon struck back. The two violently wrestled on the floor, until other congressmen pulled them apart.

The XYZ Affair

American diplomats Pinckney, Marshall, and Gerry arrived in Paris in October 1798. In time, they received a visit from three secret agents of French Foreign Minister Charles Maurice de Talleyrand-Perigord. The three agents suggested that Talleyrand would meet with the American diplomats only if he were paid a personal bribe of $250,000. The Americans were also to promise a large loan of over $10 million to France from the United States. Pinckney, Marshall, and Gerry refused to negotiate on such dishonorable terms. In answer to the demand for a bribe, General Pinckney immediately declared, "No! No! Not a sixpence."[6] They sent a full report to President Adams, substituting the letters *X*, *Y*, and *Z* for the names of the three French agents.

Adams at first hesitated to give the news of the affair to Congress. Such a report might result in a declaration of war. His message to Congress on March 19, 1798, therefore, revealed only that the diplomatic mission to France had failed.

Republicans in Congress believed Adams was holding back information favorable to the French. On April 2, 1798, the House of Representatives voted 65 to 27 demanding that Adams reveal the full text he had received. They were stunned when Adams released the documents the next day. Angry Americans snatched up newspapers to read about the shameful XYZ Affair. People yelled the slogan "Millions for defense but not one cent for tribute!"[7] These words expressed their desire for the United States to refuse to pay so much as a penny in bribes. Instead, the nation should invest money in its army and navy. Hatred of all things French swept over the country like a dark cloud. Even

In 1798, French Foreign Minister Charles Maurice de Talleyrand-Perigord secretly demanded that American diplomats pay him a huge bribe before he would agree to meet with them.

many Republicans agreed that the French had gone too far.

The United States began to prepare for war. On April 8, 1798, Congress passed new laws. The laws called for the arming of merchant ships, the construction of harbor forts, and the building of cannon factories. In May, Congress also passed a law allowing American warships to capture French ships sailing in American waters. That spring, Adams signed another law creating a new Navy Department, separate from the War Department. He appointed Benjamin Stoddert of Maryland the first secretary of the Navy.

During this time of national crisis, Adams's popularity soared. People cheered him in the streets. Yet peace, not war, remained his aim. "I should be happy in the friendship of France upon honorable conditions," he said in a letter to the citizens of Hartford, Connecticut.[8]

The Alien and Sedition Acts

As the nation got ready for war in the summer of 1798, Congress passed several laws known as the Alien and Sedition Acts. The Alien and Sedition Acts were to stay in effect for two years. One of these laws extended the residence requirement for American citizenship from five to fourteen years. Another gave the president the power to arrest or deport dangerous foreigners during wartime. Dangerous foreigners could be thrown in prison or sent out of the country.

The Sedition Act called for fines of up to $5,000 and prison terms for as long as five years for anyone "who shall by writing, printing, or speaking, threaten any person holding an office under the government, with damage to his character, person or estate."[9] Suddenly, it was illegal to speak out against the president or Congress. The First Amendment to the Constitution guaranteed freedom of speech. The Federalists who controlled Congress, however, insisted that the Sedition Act was necessary in wartime. During the next months, a dozen Republican newspaper editors were arrested and convicted under the law. Adams had not asked for the Alien and Sedition Acts. But he admitted, "I knew there was need enough . . . and therefore I consented to them."[10]

War Preparations

The undeclared war against France came to be called the Quasi-War, or Half-War. On July 2, 1798, President Adams nominated George Washington as Commander in Chief of the new army of 10,000 troops being enlisted. In a matter of days, Congress approved the nomination. Washington suggested that Alexander Hamilton be his second-in-command, with the rank of major general. Secretary of War McHenry and Secretary of State Pickering strongly supported the idea. As loyal Federalist followers of Hamilton, McHenry and Pickering saw this as a chance to make Hamilton more powerful.

On September 25, Adams reluctantly accepted Washington's choice of Hamilton. But he hoped that events in Europe might prevent the need for war altogether. In August, British Admiral Lord Horatio Nelson had destroyed the French fleet at the Battle of the Nile. Nelson's victory made France much less of a military threat. In January 1799, Adams's son Thomas arrived in Philadelphia after four years in Europe. Thomas brought news that comforted his father. At last, the French were ready to negotiate with the United States on honorable terms.

A Bold Decision

On February 18, 1799, Adams sent a brief message to the Senate. He boldly announced his nomination of William Vans Murray, the American minister to the Netherlands, to become the new minister to France. Vans Murray's mission would be to make peace. Both Republicans and Federalists were stunned by

Adams's unexpected decision. Secretary of War McHenry and Secretary of State Pickering tried to persuade Adams not to carry out this idea. A successful mission to France would ruin the Federalist party's desire for war. Adams refused to accept their advice.

A few days later, Adams realized that Vans Murray might need help. He agreed to send two additional diplomats to France, Chief Justice Oliver Ellsworth and former Virginia governor Patrick Henry. When poor health prevented Henry from going, North Carolina Governor William Davie was chosen to replace him.

Adams truly hoped the mission would be a success. But in Massachusetts, some upset Federalists claimed that had the President's "old woman" been with him in Philadelphia none of this would have happened. She would have advised for war. Abigail heard this rumor and wrote to her husband, "The old woman can tell them they are mistaken."[11]

Days of Sadness

In the autumn of 1799, John and Abigail learned for the first time that their son Charles was an alcoholic. His drinking had ruined him. "All is lost, poor, poor, unhappy wretched man," Abigail grieved.[12] His health destroyed, Charles

Adams died on December 1, 1800, at the age of thirty.

The nation suffered an even greater loss on December 14, 1799. Sixty-seven-year-old George Washington died of pneumonia at his Virginia estate, Mount Vernon. Church bells tolled in Philadelphia. President Adams sadly declared in a formal message to the Senate that the United States had lost "her most esteemed, beloved, and admired citizen . . . I feel myself alone, bereaved [taken] of my last brother."[13]

Political Campaigning

President Adams finally decided he had had enough of the scheming of two of his cabinet members. On May 5, 1800, he charged James McHenry with poor management of the War

Henry "Light Horse Harry" Lee

On December 26, 1799, President Adams and his wife attended a memorial service for George Washington. It took place at Philadelphia's Christ Church. During the service, Representative Henry "Light Horse Harry" Lee of Virginia praised Washington as "first in war, first in peace, first in the hearts of his countrymen, he was second to none . . ."[14] A cavalry general in the American Revolution, Henry Lee was the father of Civil War Confederate general Robert E. Lee.

Department. "You cannot, sir, remain longer in office," Adams declared.[15] On May 12, Adams also fired Secretary of State Timothy Pickering. He named Senator Samuel Dexter of Massachusetts as his new secretary of war. As secretary of state, he picked Representative John Marshall of Virginia. Many Federalists raged that Adams was ruining their political party. Alexander Hamilton called Adams "unfit for a President."[16]

Election fever swept the nation in the fall of 1800. Republicans chose Thomas Jefferson as their candidate for president, with New York Senator Aaron Burr as his running mate. The Federalists supported John Adams for a second term and picked Charles Cotesworth Pinckney as his running mate. Once good friends, Adams and Jefferson had become political enemies. For the only time in history, the president of the United States would be running for reelection against his own vice president.

During the campaign, Adams was cursed as a lover of royalty, more British than American. Republicans called him the "Duke of Braintree."[17] They told a false story that he once had planned to marry one of his sons to a daughter of King George III in order to reunite America and England. The Philadelphia *Aurora* blamed Adams for the new taxes, the Alien and Sedition Acts, the standing army, and a number of other "menaces."[18]

Adams received little support from Alexander Hamilton's Federalist followers. Hamilton believed that Adams was even worse than Jefferson. "If we must have an enemy at the head of the Government," Hamilton told fellow Federalists, "let it be one whom we can oppose, and for whom we are not responsible. . . ."[19]

Hamilton published a fifty-four-page pamphlet entitled "A Letter from Alexander Hamilton, Concerning the Public Conduct and Character of John Adams, Esq., President of the United States." The pamphlet openly attacked Adams. Republicans were thrilled to discover Hamilton's hatred of Adams had split the Federalist party.

Adams realized Hamilton's pamphlet deeply hurt his chances for reelection. "Mr. Hamilton has carried his eggs to a fine market," he wrote. "The very two men of all the world that he was most jealous of are now placed over him."[20] The American people had to choose between Adams and Jefferson. Hamilton hated both choices, but one of the two would be elected president.

The Executive Mansion

In October 1800, Adams traveled south to the new District of Columbia. The capital city under construction there had been renamed Washington in honor of George Washington. On November 1,

1800, Adams became the first president of the United States to sleep in the Executive Mansion.

Abigail followed him to Washington a few weeks later. She was not impressed with what she saw. "Houses scattered over a space of ten miles, and trees and stumps in plenty," she described.[21] Carpenters and plasterers still worked each day at the Executive Mansion. "No body can form an Idea of it, but those who come into it," Abigail declared. "Not one room or chamber is finished of the whole."[22] For a time, Abigail used the great unfinished East Room as a laundry room where she hung clothes to dry. The front staircase remained unfinished, too. Adams and Abigail climbed the servants' backstairs to get to their second floor chambers. Yet they never complained about their living arrangements. They realized that the "White House," as it would come to be called, would be a fine mansion when completed.

The Election of 1800

In November 1800, Adams's anxious wait for news from France ended at last. His diplomats had succeeded. A new peace treaty with France had been signed on October 3, 1800. The Quasi-War was over. For the rest of his life, Adams would be proudest of this great success. "I desire no other [words on] my gravestone," he later declared,

A White House Blessing

The White House

On November 2, 1800, after his first night in the White House, John Adams wrote Abigail a letter. In it, he offered a simple prayer: "I pray Heaven to bestow the best of Blessings on this House and all that shall hereafter inhabit it. May none but honest and wise men ever rule under this roof."[23] In the 1930s, President Franklin Delano Roosevelt had these words carved on the mantel of the State Dining Room.

"than: 'Here lies John Adams, who took upon himself the responsibility of the peace with France in the year 1800.'"[24]

The news of peace had come too late to help Adams's election campaign. On November 22, 1800, Congress gathered in Washington, D.C., for the first time. In the unfinished Capitol, Adams delivered what he knew would be his last speech as president. "I congratulate the people of the United States," he declared, "on the assembling of Congress at the permanent seat of their government. . . ."[25]

On December 3, 1800, the electors gathered to cast their ballots for president. It seemed clear that Thomas Jefferson had won. "Be not concerned for me," Adams calmly wrote to his son, Thomas, "I feel my shoulders relieved from the burden."[26] At the Capitol, on February 11, Vice President Jefferson opened the electoral ballots and announced their contents. Jefferson had received 73 votes, Adams 65, and Pinckney 64. But in a surprise twist, Jefferson's running mate, Aaron Burr, had also received 73 votes. All the Republican electors had given their second votes to Burr. As a result, Burr was tied with Jefferson. The election, according to the Constitution, would have to be decided in the House of Representatives.

Breaking the Deadlock

The very day Vice President Jefferson announced the election tie, members of the House of Representatives began the balloting process to choose the president. Each of the sixteen states had one vote. (Tennessee had joined the nation in 1796.) But if the votes of the state's representatives were evenly split, the state was to cast a blank ballot. Many Federalist congressmen favored Aaron Burr simply because they disliked Jefferson so much. On the first ballot, Jefferson failed to get the nine votes necessary to win the election. Eight states voted for him and six for Burr. The other two were evenly divided and did not vote.

Tension over the Jefferson-Burr deadlock increased during the next six days of balloting. "Things must take their course," commented Adams about the situation.[27] It had been assumed that Jefferson was the Republicans' candidate for president. But Burr refused to give up the chance to grab the office. It was whispered that Burr was secretly bargaining with the Federalists for votes. Alexander Hamilton hated both men, but in the end, he gave his support to Jefferson. "Mr. Jefferson, though too revolutionary in his notions, is yet a lover of liberty . . ." Hamilton exclaimed. "Mr. Burr loves nothing but himself. . . . In the choice of evils. . . . Jefferson is in my view less dangerous than Burr."[28] On February 17, on the thirty-sixth ballot, Jefferson finally obtained the votes of nine states. He would follow John Adams as third president of the United States. To avoid future presidential election ties, in 1804 the states would ratify the Twelfth Amendment to the Constitution. This amendment provided separate ballots when voting for president and vice president.

Final Days in Office

On February 13, 1801, Congress had passed a law creating twenty-three new federal judgeships. Adams spent his last weeks in office nominating judges to fill these positions. As his term neared its end, Adams made one of the most important decisions of his presidency. Oliver Ellsworth resigned as chief justice of the Supreme Court. To replace him, Adams appointed Secretary of State John Marshall. Marshall would serve as chief justice for thirty-four years. During that time, Marshall would guide the Supreme Court to many historic legal decisions.

On his last day in office, Adams worked at his desk late into the evening. That night, he did not go to bed. Instead, he finished packing his trunks. On inauguration day, March 4, 1801, sixty-four-year-old John Adams climbed aboard a public stagecoach at four o'clock in the morning. Tiredly, he departed Washington, D.C. He refused to attend Thomas Jefferson's inauguration at the Capitol.

Adams was proud of his accomplishments as president. He was leaving behind a nation, he said, with "fair prospects of peace . . . its commerce flourishing, its navy glorious, its agriculture uncommonly productive. . . ."[29] Despite political strife, he had always been honest, independent, and devoted to his country. "You were the man," John Quincy reminded his father, "not of any party, but of the whole nation."[30]

The Final Years

"THE ONLY QUESTION remaining with me is what shall I do with myself?" Adams wrote to a friend.[1] He arrived home at Quincy on March 18, 1801. By this time, the Adams estate included three farms altogether. They contained more than 600 acres of pastures, fields, and woods.

Farmer Adams

Each morning, Adams supervised his farm laborers as they plowed the earth and planted crops. In the afternoons, he could often be found reading in his upstairs library. He relaxed in his armchair with his favorite books. He smoked his pipe and read, while his pet dog Juno wagged her tail beside him. "Your father," Abigail told Thomas, "appears to enjoy a tranquility and a freedom of care which he has never before experienced. His books and farm occupy his attention."[2]

Sally Adams, the widow of their son Charles, and her two children came to live with Adams. Nabby Adams Smith and her four children also visited during the summers. The house in Quincy was always full of family.

The Rise of John Quincy Adams

John Quincy Adams, his wife Louisa Catherine, and their baby son returned to the United States from Europe in September 1801. Massachusetts

A Duel at Weehawken

On July 11, 1804, Alexander Hamilton and Vice President Aaron Burr met on the rocky heights beside the Hudson River at Weehawken, New Jersey. After years of political feuding, Burr had challenged Hamilton to a duel with pistols. In the exchange of gunfire, Hamilton fell fatally wounded. He died the next day in New York City. Even in death, Adams refused to forgive Hamilton. Hamilton, after all, had spoiled his chance to be elected to a second term as president.

Alexander Hamilton

citizens had grown to admire and respect John Quincy. In February 1803, they elected him to the Senate. Senator Adams soon proved his independence by being the only New England Federalist to support the Louisiana Purchase in 1803.

France and Great Britain were still at war in 1808. On the high seas, both the French and the British repeatedly seized neutral American ships and impressed American sailors. Determined to avoid war, President Jefferson called for a trade embargo. It was a measure John Quincy Adams supported. The embargo closed the port of Boston and cost Massachusetts sailors their jobs. Angry at Adams's position, in 1808 the Massachusetts legislature elected another person to succeed him in the Senate before his term was finished. Deeply insulted, Senator Adams resigned immediately.

John Adams comforted his brilliant son. "I have great confidence in your success in the service of your country, however dark your prospects may be at present. Such talents and such learning as you possess, with a character so perfectly fair . . . it is impossible for you to fail."[3] In 1809, President James Madison chose John Quincy Adams to be American minister to Russia.

Historic Letters

John Adams and Thomas Jefferson had not spoken to one another since the bitter election of 1800. Yet Adams insisted, "I always loved Jefferson, and still love him."[4] On January 1, 1812, Adams decided to write a short letter to Jefferson wishing him many happy new years. By return mail, Jefferson responded, "A letter from you calls up recollections very dear to my mind. It carries me back to the times when, beset with difficulties and dangers, we were fellow laborers in the same cause, struggling for what is most valuable to man, his right of self-government."[5]

Adams wrote back to Jefferson, "You and I ought not to die before we have explained ourselves to each other."[6] For the rest of their lives, letters traveled between the two old patriots, who wrote of common friends, shared memories, politics, philosophy, religion, their families, their health, and often the American Revolution. Jefferson's

Although once political enemies, John Adams and Thomas Jefferson (pictured) became friends again in 1812. For the rest of their lives, they corresponded through letters.

letters expressed deep thought and were written with elegant style. Adams wrote honestly and casually, his brilliant mind jumping from subject to subject. Adams greatly enjoyed hearing from Jefferson. "While you live," he cheerfully explained, "I seem to have a Bank at [Monticello] on which I can draw for a Letter of Friendship and entertainment when I please."[7]

The War of 1812

By boarding American ships at sea and impressing sailors, Great Britain continued to insult the United States. Finally, on June 19, 1812, the United States declared war on Great Britain. Each day, Adams scanned the newspapers for the latest news of sea battles and frontier skirmishes.

In July 1813, Nabby Adams Smith arrived at Quincy from her home in upstate New York. Her husband had just been elected to Congress and was in Washington, D.C. But forty-nine-year-old Nabby had cancer, and she wished to spend her last days in her parents' home. She died on August 15, 1813.

On April 1, 1814, at St. Petersburg, Russia, John Quincy Adams received word from President Madison. He had been appointed to help negotiate peace with Great Britain. Adams was to journey to Ghent in Flanders (present-day

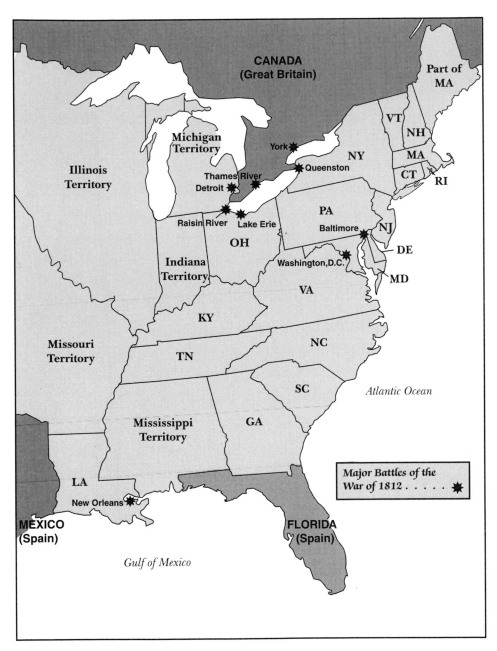

This map depicts the major battles of the War of 1812, which was fought mainly in the northern United States and southern Canada.

Belgium). By a twist of fate, it was the same important responsibility his father had had in Paris in 1783. The war was not going well for the United States. On August 24, 1814, British troops landed in Maryland and marched into Washington, D.C., where they burned the Capitol and the White House.

President Madison asked John Adams for advice. "All I can say," wrote Adams in a letter, "is, that I would continue this war forever, rather than surrender one acre of territory . . . or one sailor impressed from any merchant ship."[8] Adams was reluctant to force this opinion on his diplomat son. But he hoped that President Madison would order John Quincy to follow this advice.

When he arrived at Ghent, John Quincy Adams joined fellow American diplomats Albert Gallatin, James A. Bayard, Henry Clay, and Jonathan Russell. The Americans met with British diplomats headed by Lord James Gambier. On December 24, 1814, they successfully signed the Treaty of Ghent. Before the news of peace could reach the United States, American soldiers commanded by General Andrew Jackson won a stunning victory, on January 15, 1815, at the Battle of New Orleans.

In 1815, John Quincy Adams moved on to London. Again he was following in his father's footsteps. President Madison had named him minister to Great Britain. When James Monroe became fifth president of the United States in 1817, Monroe picked John Quincy Adams to become his secretary of state. Abigail proudly wrote him, "The voice of the nation calls you home. The government calls you home—and your parents unite in the call."[9]

Dear Partner

In October 1818, Abigail Adams fell seriously ill with typhoid fever. Adams wrote to Jefferson,

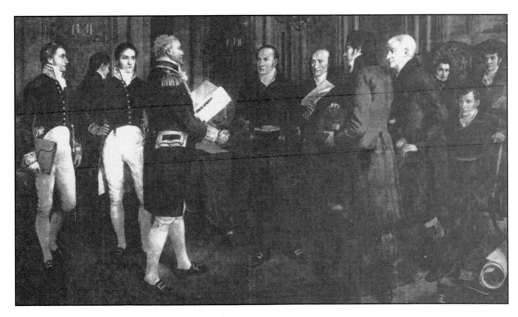

This painting depicts the signing of the Treaty of Ghent on December 24, 1814. John Quincy Adams (shaking hands with British Admiral Lord Gambier) headed the team of American diplomats that negotiated the end of the War of 1812.

"The dear Partner of my Life for fifty four Years as a Wife and for many Years more as a Lover, now [lies near death]. . . ."[10] It grieved Adams greatly to sit at her bedside. "I wish I could lay down beside her and die, too," he insisted.[11] On October 28, 1818, Abigail died at the age of seventy-three.

Thomas Jefferson sent Adams a letter of sympathy. "I know well, and feel what you have lost, what you have suffered, are suffering, and have yet to endure."[12] All Quincy was in mourning. "The tidings of her illness were heard with grief in every house, and her death is felt as a common loss," the Reverend Peter Whitney declared at Abigail's funeral service.[13]

During this time, Thomas Adams was having a difficult time earning a living. Adams insisted that Thomas become manager of the Quincy farms. Thomas soon moved into Peacefield with his wife and five children.

Even in old age, Adams remained remarkably healthy. He rose at five in the morning and would read through much of the day. He could still ride horseback in 1820 at the age of eighty-four. He often walked as much as three miles a day. Although he was bald, his teeth were gone, and he was going deaf, John Adams was still full of life.

Old friends and respectful strangers often visited Adams. "In the evening I . . . [went] to the President's and found the old gentleman well and lively," family friend Josiah Quincy once commented.[14] The summers when John Quincy and Louisa Catherine returned home to Peacefield made old John Adams the happiest.

President John Quincy Adams

In 1824, New Englanders nominated John Quincy Adams as their candidate for president. The candidates that year also included William Crawford of Georgia, Henry Clay of Kentucky, and Andrew Jackson of Tennessee. Although Andrew Jackson received more popular votes, no candidate had a majority in the electoral count. So again the decision was left to the House of Representatives. During the balloting, Speaker of the House Henry Clay threw his support behind John Quincy Adams.

Tears of joy rolled down John Adams's cheeks when he learned the news of his son's election. On March 4, 1825, at the Capitol, John Quincy Adams took the oath of office as the sixth president of the United States. Nearly fifty years had passed since John Adams had helped the United States declare its independence. By 1826, there were twenty-four states in the nation. The population was nearly 12 million—four times the size it had been in 1776.

Death of a Patriot

July 4, 1826, would mark the fiftieth anniversary of the Declaration of Independence. Ninety-year-old John Adams, eighty-three-year-old Thomas Jefferson, and eighty-eight-year-old Charles Carroll of Maryland were the last signers of the Declaration of Independence still

I had rather go forward and meet whatever is to come—I have met in this life with great trials—I have had a father and lost him—I have had a mother and lost her—I have had a wife and lost her—I have had children and lost them—I have had honorable and worthy friends and lost them—and instead of suffering these grieves again, I had rather go forward and meet my destiny.[15]

On December 1, 1825, John Adams wrote a letter to Thomas Jefferson on the subject of death.

alive. All three men were in poor health, but Adams was determined to live to see one last Fourth of July.

On June 30, 1826, a committee of Quincy town leaders called upon Adams. They asked the old patriot for a toast that they could deliver at Quincy's Fourth of July celebration.

"I will give you," Adams said, "INDEPEN-DENCE FOREVER."

When asked if he wished to add something further, he firmly replied, "Not a word."[16]

By July 4, Adams was so weak he was unable to rise from bed. At dawn, he awakened and a servant asked him, "Do you know, sir, what day this is?"

"Oh yes," softly responded Adams, "it is the glorious Fourth of July. God bless it. God bless you all."[17]

He soon fell into unconsciousness, but about one o'clock he awakened again and feebly exclaimed, "Thomas Jefferson survives!"[18]

Unknown to Adams, Thomas Jefferson had died at Monticello earlier that very day. It is said these were Adams's last words. Just before six o'clock that evening, ninety-year-old John Adams took his last breath and died.

Many people thought it a strange coincidence that Adams and Jefferson should both die exactly fifty years after the first Independence

Day. Throughout the nation, flags were flown at half-mast. Cannons boomed in salute, bells were rung, and people wore black mourning clothes. Memorial speeches praising Adams and Jefferson were delivered throughout the country. On July 7, John Adams was buried beside his wife, in the graveyard of the First Congregational Church in Quincy.

A Founding Father

Surely John Adams holds a place among the greatest of the founding fathers. During the American Revolution, Adams never fought upon a battlefield. But he fought nevertheless, and he accomplished amazing things.

As a member of the Continental Congress, it was John Adams who nominated George Washington to be Commander in Chief of the Continental Army. During months of hard debate, it was Adams who led the fight in favor of independence from Great Britain. When it came time to sign the Declaration of Independence, Adams gladly added his signature to the historic document.

Adams became one of the first diplomats to represent the new United States in foreign countries. In France and the Netherlands, Adams fought to gain support for the American war effort. He performed his duty with dignity and

John Adams (pictured) lived long enough to witness the fiftieth Independence Day on July 4, 1826.

honesty. In 1783, he joined Benjamin Franklin and John Jay in signing the Treaty of Paris. That document officially won the United States its independence. Then Adams continued to serve the nation. He became the first American minister to Great Britain. By 1788, John Adams was so highly respected that he was elected first vice president of the United States.

George Washington served two terms as president, with Adams as his vice president. But in 1796, Washington refused to run for a third term. The American people then chose John Adams to take Washington's place. In those early days of the United States, it was uncertain if the country could survive without Washington to lead it. As second president of the United States, Adams successfully guided the nation forward. He became the first president to live in the White House. He kept America out of a war with France. He chose John Marshall to become chief justice of the Supreme Court.

No one can describe American history between 1774 and 1801 without including John Adams. "You stand nearly alone in the history of our public men," Benjamin Rush, a signer of the Declaration of Independence, had once told Adams.[19] Adams lived long enough to see America grow into a strong young nation. He died knowing the country he had devotedly served would surely endure. When we look back upon our history, we can never forget the special part the Massachusetts patriot played. As one of America's founding fathers, John Adams started the United States along the path to greatness.

Timeline

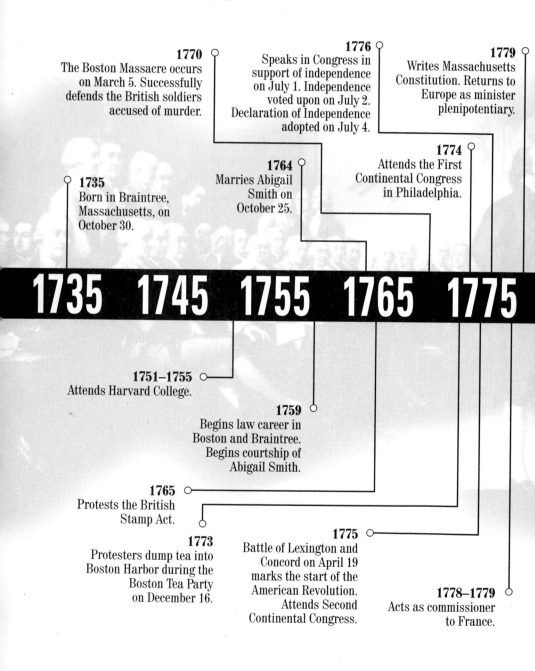

1770
The Boston Massacre occurs on March 5. Successfully defends the British soldiers accused of murder.

1776
Speaks in Congress in support of independence on July 1. Independence voted upon on July 2. Declaration of Independence adopted on July 4.

1779
Writes Massachusetts Constitution. Returns to Europe as minister plenipotentiary.

1774
Attends the First Continental Congress in Philadelphia.

1735
Born in Braintree, Massachusetts, on October 30.

1764
Marries Abigail Smith on October 25.

1735 1745 1755 1765 1775

1751–1755
Attends Harvard College.

1759
Begins law career in Boston and Braintree. Begins courtship of Abigail Smith.

1765
Protests the British Stamp Act.

1773
Protesters dump tea into Boston Harbor during the Boston Tea Party on December 16.

1775
Battle of Lexington and Concord on April 19 marks the start of the American Revolution. Attends Second Continental Congress.

1778–1779
Acts as commissioner to France.

1783
Signs Treaty of
Paris with Benjamin
Franklin and John
Jay on September 3,
ending the
Revolutionary War.

1798
XYZ Affair causes threat
of war with France. The Alien
and Sedition Acts passed.

1812
Begins exchanging friendly
letters with Thomas Jefferson.
War is declared against
Great Britain.

1826
Dies at the age of ninety on
July 4, the fiftieth anniversary
of Independence Day. Thomas
Jefferson dies on same day.

1789–1797
Serves as vice
president of
the United States.

1801
Defeated for reelection
by Thomas Jefferson.
Appoints John Marshall
Chief Justice of
the Supreme Court.
Retires to Peacefield.

1818
Abigail Adams
dies on
October 28.

1785 1795 1805 1815 1825

1785–1788
Acts as minister
to Great Britain.

1797
Elected second president
of the United States on
February 8. Takes oath
of office on March 4.

1825
John Quincy Adams
takes oath as
sixth president of
the United States.

1800
Treaty of peace
signed with
France on
October 3.
First president to
sleep in the
White House
on November 1.

1814
John Quincy Adams assists
in arranging the Treaty of Ghent,
ending the War of 1812.

1782
Establishes United States
Embassy in the Netherlands
and obtains Dutch loan.

Chapter Notes

Chapter 1. Decision in Philadelphia

1. David McCullough, *John Adams* (New York: Simon & Schuster, 2001), p. 126.

2. Ibid., p. 127.

3. Page Smith, *John Adams* (New York: Doubleday, 1962), p. 268.

4. Paul F. Boller, Jr., *Presidential Anecdotes* (England: Penguin Books Ltd., 1981), p. 30.

5. Francis Russell, *Adams: An American Dynasty* (New York: American Heritage Publishing Co., Inc., 1976), p. 71.

6. Joseph J. Ellis, *Passionate Sage: The Character and Legacy of John Adams* (New York: W. W. Norton & Company, 1993), p. 38.

7. Ibid., p. 100.

8. Gilbert Chinard, *Honest John Adams* (Gloucester, Mass., Peter Smith, 1976), pp. 126–127.

Chapter 2. Massachusetts Lawyer

1. David McCullough, *John Adams* (New York: Simon & Schuster, 2001), p. 414.

2. Ibid., p. 33.

3. Robert A. East, *John Adams* (Boston: Twayne Publishers, 1979), p. 19.

4. Ibid., p. 16.

5. Richard Brookhiser, *America's First Dynasty: The Adamses, 1735–1918* (New York: The Free Press, 2002), p. 15.

6. McCullough, p. 36.

7. Francis Russell, *Adams: An American Dynasty* (New York: American Heritage Publishing, Co., Inc., 1976), p. 20.

8. L. H. Butterfield, ed., *Diary and Autobiography of John Adams* (Cambridge, Mass.: Harvard University Press, 1961), vol. I, p. 22.

9. Gilbert Chinard, *Honest John Adams* (Gloucester, Mass.: Peter Smith, 1976), p. 27.

10. McCullough, p. 43.

11. Paul C. Nagel, *Descent From Glory* (England: Oxford University Press, 1983), p. 13.

12. Butterfield, p. 193.

13. Nagel, p. 17.

14. McCullough, p. 60.

15. Ibid., p. 61.

16. Butterfield, p. 263.

17. L. H. Butterfield, ed., *Adams Family Correspondence* (Cambridge, Mass.: Harvard University Press, 1963), vol. I, p. 83.

18. Thomas J. Fleming, "Verdicts of History I: The Boston Massacre," *American Heritage*, December 1966, p. 9.

19. Ibid., pp. 109–110.

20. McCullough, p. 68.

21. John T. Morse, *John Adams* (Boston: Houghton Mifflin Company, 1898), p. 39.

22. Chinard, p. 63.

23. Russell, p. 57.

24. Butterfield, *Adams Family Correspondence*, p. 107.

Chapter 3. A Patriot in Congress

1. John T. Morse, *John Adams* (Boston: Houghton Mifflin Company, 1898), p. 52.

2. Ibid., pp. 62–63.

3. Ibid., p. 73.

4. Gilbert Chinard, *Honest John Adams* (Gloucester, Mass.: Peter Smith, 1976), p. 77.

5. L. H. Butterfield, ed., *Adams Family Correspondence* (Cambridge, Mass.: Harvard University Press, 1963), vol. I, p. 162.

6. Ibid., p. 166.

7. Morse, p. 94.

8. Ibid., p. 96.

9. Chinard, p. 84.

10. Morse, p. 106.

11. David McCullough, *John Adams* (New York: Simon & Schuster, 2001), pp. 89–90.

12. Ibid., p. 96.

13. Ibid., p. 98.

14. Ibid., p. 76.

15. Andrew Carroll, ed., *Letters of a Nation* (New York: Kodansha International, 1997), p. 60.

16. McCullough, p. 123.

17. Richard Brookhiser, *America's First Dynasty: The Adamses, 1735–1918* (New York: The Free Press, 2002), p. 28.

18. Joseph J. Ellis, *Founding Brothers: The Revolutionary Generation* (New York: Alfred A. Knopf, 2000), p. 212.

19. Joseph J. Ellis, *Passionate Sage: The Character and Legacy of John Adams* (New York: W. W. Norton & Company, 1993), p. 113.

20. Ellis, *Founding Brothers: The Revolutionary Generation*, p. 183.

21. McCullough, p. 119.

22. National Archives and Records Administration, "Declaration of Independence," n.d. <www.nara.gov> (February 3, 2003).

23. Butterfield, p. 120.

24. McCullough, p. 163.

25. Francis Russell, *Adams: An American Dynasty* (New York: American Heritage Publishing Co., Inc., 1976), p. 75.

Chapter 4. Foreign Diplomat

1. Francis Russell, *Adams: An American Dynasty* (New York: American Heritage Publishing Co., Inc., 1976), p. 79.

2. Gilbert Chinard, *Honest John Adams* (Gloucester, Mass.: Peter Smith, 1976), p. 122.

3. Robert J. Taylor, ed., *Papers of John Adams* (Cambridge, Mass.: Belknap Press of Harvard University Press, 1983), vol. VI, p. 354.

4. Russell, p. 81.

5. Ibid., p. 80.

6. Richard Brookhiser, *America's First Dynasty: The Adamses*, 1735–1918 (New York: The Free Press, 2002), p. 7.

7. Chinard, p. 124.

8. David McCullough, *John Adams* (New York: Simon & Schuster, 2001), p. 221.

9. Ibid., p. 225.

10. Ibid., p. 229.

11. L. H. Butterfield, ed., *Adams Family Correspondence* (Cambridge, Mass.: Harvard University Press, 1963), vol. III, p. 243.

12. Ibid., p. 252.

13. John T. Morse, *John Adams* (Boston: Houghton Mifflin Company, 1898), p. 194.

14. Robert A. East, *John Adams* (Boston: Twayne Publishers, 1979), p. 63.

15. Chinard, pp. 174–175.

16. McCullough, p. 285.

17. Russell, p. 94.

18. Lida Mayo, "Miss Adams In Love," *American Heritage*, February 1965, p. 82.

19. McCullough, p. 335.

20. Butterfield, vol. VI, p. 347.

21. Mayo, p. 81.

22. Julian Boyd, ed., *The Papers of Thomas Jefferson* (Princeton, N.J.: Princeton University Press, 1950), vol. VIII, p. 548.

23. McCullough, p. 383.

24. Ibid., p. 349.

25. Ibid., p. 391.

Chapter 5. First Vice President of the United States

1. David McCullough, *John Adams* (New York: Simon & Schuster, 2001), pp. 401–402.

2. Ibid., p. 412.

3. Ibid., p. 425.

4. Ibid., p. 406.

5. Robert C. Alberts, "The Cantankerous Mr. Maclay," *American Heritage*, October 1974, p. 84.

6. Gilbert Chinard, *Honest John Adams* (Gloucester, Mass.: Peter Smith, 1976), p. 228.

7. McCullough, p. 431

8. Ibid., p. 399.

9. Ibid., p. 422.

10. Julian Boyd, ed., *The Papers of Thomas Jefferson* (Princeton, N.J.: Princeton University Press, 1950), vol. XXIII, pp. 538–539.

11. McCullough, pp. 444–445.

12. Ibid., p. 447.

13. Ibid.

14. Ibid., p. 454.

15. Ibid., p. 462.

16. Chinard, p. 256.

Chapter 6. Second President of the United States

1. Paul F. Boller, Jr., *Presidential Anecdotes* (England: Penguin Books Ltd., 1981), p. 24.

2. David McCullough, *John Adams* (New York: Simon & Schuster, 2001), p. 471.

3. Ibid., p. 476.

4. Gilbert Chinard, *Honest John Adams* (Gloucester, Mass.: Peter Smith, 1976), p. 265.

5. Joseph J. Ellis, *Founding Brothers: The Revolutionary Generation* (New York: Alfred A. Knopf, 2000), p. 185.

6. Alexander DeConde, *The Quasi-War* (New York: Scribner, 1966), p. 49.

7. Francis Russell, *Adams: An American Dynasty* (New York: American Heritage Publishing Co., Inc., 1976), p. 126.

8. McCullough, p. 501.

9. Russell, p. 127.

10. McCullough, p. 505.

11. Ellis, p. 192.

12. Paul C. Nagel, *Descent From Glory* (England: Oxford University Press, 1983), p. 79.

13. McCullough, pp. 532–533.

14. Ralph L. Woods, ed., *A Treasury of the Familiar* (Chicago: Consolidated Book Publishers, 1944), p. 658.

15. Harold C. Syrett, ed., *Papers of Alexander Hamilton* (New York: Columbia University Press, 1974), vol. XXIV, p. 564.

16. Russell, p. 128.

17. Chinard, p. 305.

18. McCullough, p. 544.

19. Paul F. Boller, Jr., *Presidential Campaigns* (New York: Oxford University Press, 1984), pp. 10–11.

20. *The American Heritage Pictorial History of the Presidents of the United States* (New York: American Heritage Publishing Co., Inc., 1968), vol. I, p. 72.

21. Russell, p. 130.

22. Ibid.

23. *The American Heritage Pictorial History of the Presidents of the United States*, p. 72.

24. Chinard, p. 312.

25. McCullough, p. 554.

26. Ibid., pp. 555–556.

27. Ibid., p. 562.

28. Ibid., pp. 557–558.

29. Ibid., p. 566.

30. Nagel, p. 81.

Chapter 7. The Final Years

1. David McCullough, *John Adams* (New York: Simon & Schuster, 2001), p. 568.

2. Ibid., p. 571.

3. Ibid., pp. 587–588.

4. Lester J. Cappon, ed., *The Adams-Jefferson Letters* (Chapel Hill: The University of North Carolina Press, 1959), vol. II 1812–1826, p. 284.

5. Ibid., p. 291.

6. Francis Russell, *Adams: An American Dynasty* (New York: American Heritage Publishing Co., Inc., 1976), p. 136.

7. Cappon, p. 530.

8. Joseph J. Ellis, *Passionate Sage: The Character and Legacy of John Adams* (New York: W. W. Norton & Company, 1993), p. 112.

9. McCullough, p. 620.

10. Cappon, p. 529.

11. Paul C. Nagel, *Descent From Glory* (England: Oxford University Press, 1983), p. 130.

12. Cappon, p. 529.

13. McCullough, p. 624.

14. Ibid., p. 636.

15. Gilbert Chinard, *Honest John Adams* (Gloucester, Mass.: Peter Smith, 1976), p. 345.

16. L. H. Butterfield, "July 4 In 1826," *American Heritage*, June 1955, p. 102.

17. Paul F. Boller, Jr., *Presidential Anecdotes* (England: Penguin Books Ltd., 1981), p. 27.

18. Butterfield, pp. 102–103.

19. William A. DeGregorio, *The Complete Book of Presidents* (New York: Dembner Books, 1984), p. 32.

Glossary

abstain—To deny oneself an action.

ancestor—A person from whom one has descended; a relative from long ago.

boycott—To join with others in refusing to deal with someone, usually to show disapproval or to force acceptance of terms.

casually—In an informal manner.

commerce—The buying or selling of goods.

contrive—To devise or bring about.

customhouse—A building where taxes or duties on cargoes are collected from ships.

deacon—An officer of a church.

embargo—A government order prohibiting commerce with an enemy.

federal—Relating to a central government.

flourish—To achieve success, prosper, thrive.

garrison—A place in which military troops are regularly stationed.

impress—To take by force into naval service.

influenza—A viral disease that causes fever, aches, and difficulty breathing; commonly called "the flu."

manslaughter—The killing of a person without planning beforehand.

monarchy—A government by a single person, such as a king.

monopoly—Ownership without competition.

negotiate—To arrange or bring about something through discussion.

neutrality—A neutral or uncommitted position.

orator—A skilled public speaker.

ordnance—Military supplies including weapons, vehicles, and ammunition.

plenipotentiary—A person given full power to conduct business.

quasi—Having a resemblance to.

radical—Extreme.

ratify—To approve formally.

render—To give or deliver to.

righteous—Acting according to religious or moral law.

rotund—Marked by roundness, especially plump.

sovereign—One who exercises supreme authority.

strife—A conflict, fight, or struggle.

thatch—A sheltering cover of plant material, such as straw, reeds, etc.

tribute—A payment from one ruler or nation to another especially to gain peace.

typhoid—A bacterial disease causing fever, headache, and rash.

tyrant—An absolute ruler, often harsh.

unalienable—Something that is incapable of being alienated, surrendered, or transferred.

unanimous—Showing total agreement.

Further Reading

Feinstein, Stephen. *John Adams: A MyReportLinks.com Book*. Berkeley Heights, N.J.: Enslow Publishers, Inc., 2002.

Kallen, Stuart A. *Life During the American Revolution*. Farmington Hills, Mich.: Gale Group, 2002.

Marcovitz, Hal. *The Declaration of Independence*. Broomall, Pa.: Mason Crest Publishers, 2002.

Ready, Dee. *The Boston Massacre*. Mankato, Minn.: Capstone Press, 2002.

St. George, Judith. *John and Abigail Adams*. New York: Holiday House, 2001.

Whitehurst, Susan. *The Colony of Massachusetts*. New York: The Rosen Publishing Group, Inc., 2000.

Internet Addresses

EnchantedLearning.com. "John Adams." © 2001–2003. <http://www.enchantedlearning.com/history/us/pres/adams/>.

MultiEducator, Inc. "Causes of War." *Revolutionary War: Birth of a Nation*. © 2000. <http://www.multied.com/Revolt/causes.html>.

The White House. "Biography of John Adams." *Past Presidents*. n.d. <http://www.whitehouse.gov/history/presidents/ja2.html>.

Places to Visit

Adams National Historical Park
135 Adams Street
Quincy, Massachusetts 02169-1749
(617) 770-1175
e-mail: ADAM_Visitor_Center@nps.gov
<http://www.nps.gov/adam/>

Boston Tea Party Ship & Museum
Congress Street Bridge
Boston, Massachusetts 02110
(617) 338-1773
e-mail: bostps@historictours.com
<http://historictours.com>

Federal Hall National Memorial
26 Wall Street
New York, New York 10005
(212) 825-6888
<http://www.nps.gov/feha/>

Independence National Historical Park
313 Walnut Street
Philadelphia, PA 19106
(215) 597-8974 (visitor center)
<http://www.nps.gov/inde/>

Index